# —101— WAYS TO SAY THANK YOU

## NOTES OF GRATITUDE
### FOR
### ALL OCCASIONS

### KELLY BROWNE

FOREWORD BY
DOROTHEA JOHNSON
FOUNDER OF THE PROTOCOL SCHOOL
OF WASHINGTON®

STERLING
New York

*To my mother and father, Peggy and Richard Learman . . .*
*Whose gracious hearts have illuminated the world*
*and changed lives in ways only the stars can see.*
*With all my love, always . . .*

A portion of the author's royalties for this book has been
donated to St. Jude Children's Research Hospital.

STERLING
New York

An Imprint of Sterling Publishing
1166 Avenue of the Americas
New York, NY 10036

This revised edition published in 2015 by Sterling Publishing Co., Inc.
© 2008 by Kelly Browne. New material © 2015 by Kelly Browne

ISBN 978-1-4549-1560-7

Distributed in Canada by Sterling Publishing
c/o Canadian Manda Group, 664 Annette Street
Toronto, Ontario, Canada M6S 2C8
Distributed in the United Kingdom by GMC Distribution Services
Castle Place, 166 High Street, Lewes, East Sussex, England BN7 1XU
Distributed in Australia by Capricorn Link (Australia) Pty. Ltd.
P.O. Box 704, Windsor, NSW 2756, Australia

For information about custom editions, special sales, and premium and corporate purchases,
please contact Sterling Special Sales at 800-805-5489 or specialsales@sterlingpublishing.com.

Manufactured in the United States of America

2 4 6 8 10 9 7 5 3 1

www.sterlingpublishing.com

# FOREWORD

Hail the handwritten note! It has been around for hundreds of years, and we will not witness its demise simply because some of its everyday functions have been replaced by email and voice mail. Of course, it's a given that email and telephones are most efficient for staying in touch and handling daily communications, but when it comes to a cut above, paper and pen rule.

In this refreshed edition embracing the digital world we live in, Kelly Browne takes a modern, common sense—albeit elegant—approach to note writing. Though highly practical, this book's lively text makes it a joy to peruse. Ms. Browne's guidelines will encourage you to pick up your pen and express yourself in ways that messages delivered via telephone or email simply can't convey.

If the people of the world become a little more thoughtful about showing gratitude by writing notes, it will be in no small measure thanks to the efforts of Kelly Browne.

Dorothea Johnson
Author, Etiquette Expert and Founder of The Protocol School of Washington®

*Gratitude is the most exquisite form of courtesy.*

—JACQUES MARITAIN, FRENCH PHILOSOPHER

# ACKNOWLEDGMENTS

I'd like to thank *everyone* who made this book possible. . . . I am so humbled by the millions of people who have given the gift of gratitude and shared that magic around the globe. From the bottom of my heart—I thank you all. Linda Konner, thank you, thank you, thank you. You made all of this possible—I am *so* grateful to you always. Kate Zimmermann, Hannah Reich, and *everyone* at Sterling Publishing, past and present, thank you for being champions of this book! Charles Kittredge, Norma LeBarron, Jessica Haas, Megan Kuntze, Robert Murray, and the entire Crane & Co. team in Massachusetts, I thank you for your continued endorsement! Your gorgeous stationery on cotton paper has been a rich part of our history in expressing gratitude for hundreds of years! Dorothea Johnson, I am *forever grateful* to you for graciously helping me. Your charming gems of wisdom have changed my life—I appreciate and adore you. Pamela Eyring, my deepest thanks to you, Robert Hickey, and the Protocol School of Washington. I applaud and appreciate the work you have done in the global community to create cultures of civility. Cindy Haygood, Debra Lassiter, and April McLean of the Etiquette & Leadership Institute, your work with our young adults will be carried into the world, touching lives and spreading goodwill—thank you! All of my friends, especially Kimberly Wileman, Robin Prybil, and Lizzie Blatt—I love you. Steven Blatt, you are indeed a mensch; my deepest gratitude to you always for everything. To the magical Gary Grabel and brilliant Mark Hamermesh, I thank you. Betty Borian and Stephanie and Carolyn Mente, there are no words to express my appreciation to all of you. My family, Jack and Mick Kerrigan; Edward, William, and Gretchen Learman Burrier; and the Mullens, Kerrigan, and Fish families—my love and gratitude is with you always. My parents, Richard and Peggy Learman, thank you for every single thing— I love you both so much. Greta and Ava, my gorgeous little treasures, you are my everything. My husband, Aric, I thank God every day for the gift of sharing my life with you— I love you. And finally, St. Jude, thank you for listening.

*Give gratitude . . .*
*It is the silver thread that connects us all.*

KELLY BROWNE

# CONTENTS

# INTRODUCTION

Every young woman knows that sending the classic handwritten thank-you note is as essential as her little black dress. Now more than ever before, people are embracing the time-honored tradition of remembering the thoughtfulness of a friend, relative, or business associate with a formal note of thanks. Yes, we're all busy, but in this world of electronic communication, nothing stands out more or lets people know how much you appreciate their act of kindness than a personal, handwritten thank-you note.

If embracing your inner regal nature isn't enough or if your mother's constant reminders have not provided sufficient motivation, consider that not acknowledging someone for the gift of generosity can be hurtful. Remember your reputation before you decide your life is too hectic to say thank you. Studies have shown that when someone says thank you, it creates a chain reaction of kindness that in turn promotes a cycle of gratitude. It shouldn't be a mystery why so many philosophers and religions embrace gratitude as a valuable state of well-being. Imagine the positive global effect we could each have if we made showing our appreciation a part of our daily practice. Think about it. When you post, share, tweet, or check in, your comments have the ability to light up and inspire everyone around the world.

Starting today, commit to making a habit of daily thanking the people you encounter for the little things they do for you. You'll be amazed how much people appreciate being acknowledged for their acts of kindness. The truth is, in one small second, something magical happens when you give gratitude. It's a wave of emotion you can literally feel. So when you assume you don't have the ability to promote world peace, think again. The magic words are *please* and *thank you!*

With thanks to my mother for her insistence, I learned that a meaningful thank-you note really does make a difference, not only in the life of the person you are thanking, but also in your own. Once again, she was right. Common courtesies and true thankfulness have changed my life for the better. This book is designed to help people everywhere reap the same benefits I have—by learning to cultivate gratitude and by sharing that appreciation through thank-you notes that really can make a difference.

Inside you'll find my personal guide to the basics in "Thank-You Notes 101," as well as sample thank-you notes for everything from wedding gifts and birthday presents to those intangible gifts of support that make life so much easier during difficult times. I hope my notes will inspire you when you write your own. You'll also find a variety of "Quips" and "Tips" from "Grateful Sages" who knew the power of showing appreciation, as well as quick and easy checklists to help you say thank you with grace and style. Since we have embraced technology, I have refreshed the material throughout to include essential information on cybersecurity and using social media and digital tools to your advantage in the workplace and your personal life. To keep you dazzling in cyberspace, you'll also find a new chapter, "Netiquette 101," to guide you when you express your virtual gratitude.

It is my hope that my book will encourage you to spend a little more time counting your blessings and letting people know how much their thoughtfulness and generosity have meant to you, and that by putting your appreciation into action you make our world a better place. In the words of my ancestor Daniel Webster, American orator and statesman, "What a man does for others, not what they do for him, gives him immortality."

I challenge you to do the same.

A thousand thank-yous...

—*Kelly Browne*

"*Give, and it will be given to you . . .*
*for by your standard of measure it will be*
*measured to you in return.*"

—JESUS (LUKE 6:38)

# CHAPTER 1

## THANK-YOU NOTES 101:
## GETTING BACK TO BASICS

J ust as you are slipping into those fabulous strappy heels and heading for the door, something catches your eye. In the corner of the room sits the open box with the pink cashmere sweater Aunt Greta sent you weeks ago. Of course you meant to thank her but somehow it just never happened. If you don't do it now, chances are you'll forget about it again, and the last thing you want is for anyone to believe you are ungrateful.

Rather than come up with a list of excuses, just be the lady you truly are and write that thank-you note as graciously as possible. But where do you start?

*January 16, 2016*

*Dear Aunt Greta,*

*Thanks for the pink sweater. I like it and hope you are well.*

*Love,*

*Ava*

Not so good. Try again . . .

*January 16, 2016*

*Dear Aunt Greta,*

*Thank you so much for the gorgeous pink sweater. It looks lovely with my new skirt and is perfect for my interview next week. You always find such fabulous treasures! Thank you for making me feel so special.*

*Love,*

*Ava*

Not only is the second version much better in sentiment, but more important, when Aunt Greta opens her mailbox and reads your thank-you note, she will feel the magic sparkle of gratitude come back to her for her generosity to you.

## WRITING THE CLASSIC THANK-YOU NOTE

It's easy to write a thank-you note because the format is always the same: the date, salutation, your thank-you message, the closing, and your signature. Break it down like this:

1. Write the date.

    *January 16, 2016*

2. Write the salutation.

    *Dear (put person's name here),*

    ❋ "Dear" is the most popular salutation to use, but you can also use "Dearest" for a loved one or your own term of endearment, depending on the situation.

✽ Remember to use a comma following the salutation and addressee's name for all handwritten notes, social or casual.

✽ If you're writing a thank-you note to a couple, you can write the note to one of them and mention the other in the text of the note, or you can address it to both of them.

✽ Use "Mr. and Mrs." for formal notes and use first names for intimate and casual relationships.

3. Write the content of your thank-you note.

Thank the person for the gift as genuinely and graciously as you can. Try to add something extra like, "I look forward to seeing you soon," or "I hope you're doing well," or "My mother sends her love," or even the popular "Let's do lunch!"

4. Write the closing.

If you aren't sure what is appropriate for the situation, "Sincerely yours" is always an elegant choice and in accordance with social protocol.

**For Formal and Business Notes**

| | |
|---|---|
| Sincerely, | Very sincerely, |
| Sincerely yours, | Very sincerely yours, |

**For Thank-You Notes of Love and Friendship**

| | | |
|---|---|---|
| Affectionately, | Fondly, | Love, |
| Love always, | Truly yours, | Warmly, |
| With affection, | Your friend, | Yours, |
| Yours truly, | | |

**For Thank-You Notes for Special Gifts and Favors**

| | |
|---|---|
| Gratefully, | Gratefully yours, |

**For Thank-You Notes to Clergy and Statesmen**

Faithfully yours,    Respectfully,         Respectfully yours,

Sincerely yours,    Yours faithfully,

**For General Thank Yous**

Best regards,       Best wishes for (*insert sentiment*),

Best wishes,        My best wishes for (*insert sentiment*),

GRATEFUL SAGE TIP

According to etiquette expert Dorothea Johnson,
"Traditionally, if you want to use forms of 'best wishes'
and 'best regards,' it should be for something." For
example, "Best wishes for an amazing honeymoon."

5. Add your signature.
   Your first name, or your first and last name.

   ✦ Most commonly, people sign their first name for personal
   relationships and their full name for formal ones.

   ✦ Make sure your signature is legible. Often signatures become a
   bunch of circles or a squiggly line, and the poor recipient of your
   note is left baffled as to who you might be.

   ✦ If you write electronically and then print your thank-you
   note, you must handwrite your name.

   ✦ If your signature is illegible, you might want to use
   personalized stationery.

Your note should look like this on the page:

*January 16, 2016*

*Dear Grandma Esther,*

*Thank you for the very generous check you sent. I desperately need to get a new wireless printer for my laptop, and now I can buy one, thanks to you! Now all my papers for school will look amazing and be on time. I truly appreciate that you are always thinking of me. You are a very special person.*

*With all my love,*

*Ava*

## Six Do's for Elegant Notes

1. Do handwrite your note neatly, without mistakes, on good-quality stationery using blue or black ink. If you love the luxury and look of a fountain pen, check out disposable fountain pens.

2. Do use glowing superlatives and energetic adjectives like *fabulous, amazing, delightful,* and *extraordinary.* Be creative. Really think about the moment you opened the gift and how you felt, and then tell them about it. Be expansive and passionate, and convey your emotion.

3. Do mention in your thank-you note how you plan to use the gift. This shows that the gift was well chosen, and that's one of the best ways to say thank you.

4. Do add a compliment such as, "You have wonderful taste," or "How do you always know just what to get for me?" or "You are such a thoughtful and kind person, and I'm so grateful to have you in my life." Everybody likes to know that they are appreciated.

5. Do keep your note to a paragraph or two in length. Remember, it is a note, not a letter. You can make it longer if you want to, but it is not expected.

6. Do make each note sound special and unique to the person, situation, and gift. Thank-you notes should never feel generic.

GRATEFUL SAGE TIP

If you have trouble putting the note all together, write it out first on a piece of scrap paper, or type it up on your computer, spell-check it, then copy it neatly. For help writing in a straight line, go to my website, www. KellyBrowne.net, and download the *101 Ways to Say Thank You Lined Paper Template* to slip under your stationery.

## The Stationery Wardrobe

A "stationery wardrobe" consists of versatile stationery that you can readily use for any occasion and that gives you the opportunity to reflect your unique personality. Especially in the digital age we live in, your choice of paper, color, size, and weight makes a statement not only about you, but also about how you feel about your recipient. Stationery can be engraved, thermographed (raised printing), or flat-printed and should always suit the occasion. Whether your needs are social or business, a stationery wardrobe is a valuable tool. Typically, a wardrobe will contain:

❊ Correspondence cards (4¼″ x 6½″): The most versatile stationery for writing short notes, thank-yous, and invitations; only the front may be used. These can be printed with your monogram, crest, or name and are usually a heavier paper weight.

❊ Informals (5¼″ x 3½″): While their name might sound confusing, "informals" are actually formal notes. Folded in half and often referred to as "fold-overs," informals can be printed with your name or monogram on the front. For a level of high formality, choose paper colors like ecru or white, with your proper social name in black engraving. For example,

*Mrs. Richard Meldrum Learman*

- ❖ Single sheet stationery: Printed with your name and street address at the top, the size and weight of these papers is up to you and depends on the length and formality of your letters. If a second sheet is needed, a blank one should be used. Lighter in weight, they can fit through a printer, if necessary.

- ❖ Note sheets (6⅜″ x 8½″): Perfect for social use.

- ❖ Monarch or executive stationery (7¼″ x 10½″): These sheets are used for both social letters and personal business letters.

- ❖ Standard letter sheets (8½″ x 11″): Most frequently used for business letters.

- ❖ Envelopes: Keep in mind that stationery wardrobes are often created to make it possible to use one size envelope for several different sizes of paper. Envelopes should include a return address, but including your name is optional.

- ❖ Calling cards: Varying in size and similar to a business card, calling cards are for new acquaintances and include your personal contact information, such as your name, phone number, email address, and website or home address. You can simply use your name and phone number or your name and email address—it's up to you.

Start your stationery wardrobe with your most essential stationery pieces—one for your thank-you notes and one for writing letters.

# THE THANK YOU THESAURUS:
## GLOWING SUPERLATIVES AND ENERGETIC ADJECTIVES

Try some of these words to add a little excitement to your notes!

—◦—

amazing astonishing astounding attractive AWE-INSPIRING beautiful **beyond belief** bright brilliant colorful dazzling excellent **exceptional** extraordinary fabulous fine-looking GENEROUS gleaming glistening GLOWING good-looking gorgeous handsome hard to believe incandescent inconceivable incredible iridescent lively lovely **luminous** marvelous MIRACULOUS multi-colored out of this world outstanding radiant remarkable rich shimmering **SHINING** sparkling **spectacular** splendid STARTLING striking stunning surprising unbelievable VIBRANT vivid wonderful

# SOCIAL AND SAVVY STATIONERY FOR THE PERFECT THANK-YOU

Traditionally, the appropriate formal social stationery to use for thank-you notes is of good quality and is white or ecru in color. However, pastel colors have become not only acceptable but also popular.

* The most formal of social stationery is the traditional fold-over note, called the "informal." These can be plain or personalized with your monogram, crest, or name. When folded, they measure approximately 5¼″ x 3½″. They can also be used for invitations and short notes.

* Correspondence cards with your name or monogram printed across the top, with a small design or embellished with a border, are also popular. They are typically a heavier card stock and measure 4¼″ x 6½″ in size. Only the front side of the card is used.

* Boxes of good-quality fold-over notes that have "Thank You" or a small design printed on the cover of the flap are readily available at most stationery stores. The inside is blank for your note.

❀ There are single and boxed cards that have beautiful pictures on the front and that are blank on the inside. For example, many museums print paintings and photographs on cards and sell them in their gift shops.

❀ Thank-you cards with a preprinted inscription of thanks are also available. These are fine in casual situations where you write a personal thank-you note inside the card. It is not acceptable just to sign your name. Why? Because someone took time to do something special for you, now it is important for you to take time to thank them properly.

❀ Affordable personalized stationery wardrobes are available printed with your name and address. These can make your thank-you note writing and social correspondence easier.

## The Do's and Don'ts of Using Honorifics

1. Do remember that an *honorific* refers to titles that show respect or honor such as Mr., Mrs., Miss, and Ms.

2. Do include the appropriate honorific in the formal and business thank-you note as well as on the envelope.

3. Do use "Miss" if you are addressing a single woman in a formal or social note.

4. Do use "Ms." for professional women, divorced women resuming their maiden name, or when you are uncertain of a woman's marital status.

5. Don't use an honorific for yourself when signing your name on your thank-you note.

6. Do use "Mr. and Mrs." when addressing a married couple, followed by the husband's formal name, so it includes the first, middle, and last names: *Mr. and Mrs. Richard Meldrum Learman.*

7. Do use "Mrs." when formally addressing a married woman, followed by her husband's formal name: *Mrs. Richard Meldrum Learman.*

8. Do include "Mrs." for a divorced woman retaining her married name, followed by her first, maiden, and married names: *Mrs. Margaret Kerrigan Stark.*

9. Do use "Doctor" as either the full word or the abbreviation "Dr." when addressing a male doctor and his wife: *Dr. and Mrs. Irving Iscoe.* In addressing a husband and wife where she is the doctor, both full names can appear on the same line or hers on a separate line above his.

10. Do check the appropriate title when addressing your note to a statesman, academic, or a member of the clergy or royalty.

### GRATEFUL SAGE TIP

*The Protocol School of Washington's Honor & Respect: The Official Guide to Names, Titles, & Forms of Address* by Robert Hickey, with a foreword by Pamela Eyring, is an essential resource to refer to often for tips, guidelines, formulas, and proper forms of address. For more information, go to: www.psow.edu.

## COMPUTER-READY STATIONERY

If you decide to create your thank-you note on the computer, a vast selection of stationery is available to choose from, and it's very easy to print different sizes of paper on your printer. Use the "page setup" menu when creating your new document and adjust the page size to that of your paper and envelope. If you are creating a fold-over note, for example, you will need to click on "margins" (within the "page setup" menu) to adjust the left- and right-hand margins and also to adjust the top margin so your text will appear below the fold. Make sure you do a test run on inexpensive copy paper before using your best stationery.

You can find a wide variety of gorgeous paper, ranging from high quality to inexpensive. As long as it isn't too thick or too small for your printer, high-end preprinted personalized stationery will work and will look lovely. Watermarked, 100 percent cotton paper, which is available in varying weights, always looks more elegant than copy paper, which should never be used for thank-you notes.

### GRATEFUL SAGE TIP

Crane & Co. has an incredible selection of classic and stylish stationery from which to choose. You can order personalized, preprinted thank-you cards and all-occasion stationery online at www.Crane.com or at your local stationery store.

## AND THE ENVELOPE, PLEASE . . .

That little envelope is just as important as your thank-you note, so please don't cast it off as insignificant. Remember, it's the very first thing the recipient sees when your note arrives, and you want to make a favorable impression immediately.

Formal Envelopes: Only the addressee's name and address should be on the front of the envelope with the state name written out, not abbreviated. The return address should be written on the *back flap* of the envelope, *without* the return addressee's name.

Casual and Business Envelopes: The addressee's name should begin at the center of the envelope with the street address directly underneath it. The next line is the city, state, and zip code. Be sure to include your return address in the upper left corner of the envelope.

The front of your casual envelope should look like this:

*Your Name*
*1234 Street Avenue*
*Town, ST 90000-1234*

*Mrs. Gift Giver*
*4321 Street Avenue*
*Anytown, ST 80000-4321*

Insert your thank-you note into the envelope with the folded side up and the front of the note facing toward you, so the flap of the envelope closes down over the front of the note.

## Six Simple Do's and Don'ts for the Elegant Envelope

1. Do make sure you double-check the address before you write it on the front of the envelope.

2. Do handwrite your envelope if your note is handwritten (which is always best).

3. Don't send a typed or computer-printed thank-you note with a hand-addressed envelope. Whatever you choose, they should match.

4. Don't use stick-on address labels; they look impersonal. Putting the envelope through your printer using a script font is a better alternative.

5. Do include the last four digits of the nine-digit zip code for United States addresses, for example, 91000-1234. It will get there faster! If you don't know the full zip code, check it online at www.usps.com.

6. Do check out the variety of stamps available at your local post office or online. There are so many beautiful stamps to choose from, and they can enhace your presentation. Tip: Check out: www.photo.stamps.com to upload your image and personalize your stamp!

## Sending Your Global Gratitude—
## International Forms of Address

Always be sure to verify international addresses and ensure that they follow the formatting guidelines and conventions of the countries where you are sending your mail.

According to the United States Postal Service, all mail should include 1) the return address—which is the address of the sender—in the upper left-hand corner, and 2) the recipient's name and delivery address written to the right and center of the envelope. Both should be printed on the same side of the envelope or package using uppercase Roman letters and numbers, i.e.: ABC, 123. The standard order of the international delivery address should be addressed this way, but in some countries the format may vary.

**Line 1:** Name of addressee. Example:
*Mrs. Recipient Name*

**Line 2:** Street address or post office box number. Example:
*1234 Street Drive*

**Line 3:** City or town name, other principal subdivision (such as province, state, or county), and postal code (if known). Example:
*London WIP 6HQ*

**Line 4:** Full country name. Example:
*England*

Here are a few examples for sending international correspondence:

AUSTRALIA: **www.auspost.com.au**
Recipient's Name
House Number + Street Name
Suburb and State/Territory
Postcode
Australia

CANADA: **www.canadapost.ca**
Recipient's Name
House Number + Street Name
City, Provence, Postal Code
Canada

FRANCE: **www.laposte.fr**
Recipent's Name
House Number + Street Name
Postal Code, Town Name
France

ITALY: **www.posteitaliane.post**
Recipient's Name
Street Name + House Number
Postal Code, City, Province Code
Italy

UNITED EMIRATES: **www.epg.gov.ae**
Recipient's Name
Title and/or Company Name
P. O. Box
Emirate
UAE

UNITED KINGDOM: **www.royalmail.com**
Recipient's Name
House Number + Street Name
City/Town Name, Postal Code
(Country: Ireland/England/Wales)
United Kingdom

## HANDWRITTEN NOTES VERSUS COMPUTER-GENERATED NOTES

Traditionally, thank-you notes are handwritten neatly on good-quality stationery, have no mistakes, and are in blue or black ink. This is by far the most socially acceptable manner in which to offer a thank-you note. It is personal, gracious, and thoughtful. In today's electronic world, the handwritten note is even more treasured. However, many of us feel embarrassed by our handwriting, which can make writing a thank-you note a very intimidating and awkward situation—especially when we want to look graceful. So which is worse, not sending a thank-you note or typing one? The answer is obvious. There is absolutely no reason you cannot create your thank-you notes on your computer or mobile device if you are faced with this situation. In fact, there are several advantages if you choose to go the computer-generated route. For example, you can use the grammar and spell-check function on your word-processing application and catch errors you may have otherwise missed. Your note is neat, legible, and often better thought out, because you can delete what you wrote and start over! We are often committed to what we have started in handwritten notes because we don't want to waste the paper or write it all over again.

### GRATEFUL SAGE TIP

Look for a basic script font that looks like handwriting, but stay away from the styles that are too ornate and difficult to read.

### The Golden Rules for Timely Thank-You Success

1. Do send your thank-you note immediately; then you won't forget.

2. Do remember to send a thank-you note within two weeks of receiving a gift.

3. Do keep in mind a phone call never counts as a thank-you! A note must be sent after the call.

## DAMAGE CONTROL
## FOR LATE THANK-YOU NOTES

At some point, you will be faced with having to send a late thank-you note. Regardless of how late you are, it is still better to send one. Yes, the person may be hurt or offended that you did not show your gratefulness in a timely manner, but it will be appreciated nonetheless.

First, how late are you? If you are within days or a week or two of the reasonable time limit, don't worry about it. Send your note and don't bother to mention the delay. If, however, you are sending out a thank-you note for a wedding gift you received seven months earlier—be honest. You can explain briefly that you were late in sending it out: "While filling the gorgeous vase you gave me for our wedding with beautiful red roses, it suddenly occurred to me that I never sent you a thank-you note! Please forgive me." Then continue with your note.

You can always call or email the person to acknowledge the gift and then send a handwritten note, too. Sometimes this can help smooth a situation over, especially if you share a personal moment, for example, describing something funny that happened on your honeymoon or how you felt when you heard your baby cry for the first time.

" *Do not spoil what you have by desiring what you have not; remember that what you now have was once among the things you only hoped for.* "

—EPICURUS, GREEK PHILOSOPHER

# CHAPTER 2
## NETIQUETTE 101:
## VIRTUAL GRATITUDE

The digital revolution has changed our lives in ways we have yet to imagine. As we navigate through the electronic frontier, it is vital to remember our global connectivity and promote virtual respect. Remember, regardless of social media website claims of privacy, you are never anonymous, and how you represent yourself online is key to your success. Your Internet history of the pictures you post—or comments you make—will remain part of your digital footprint and can impact future jobs and opportunities. Now more than ever, we must respect our differences, promote gratitude, celebrate love, and learn from one another, for we are truly citizens of the world. Take a moment and embrace your virtual gratitude when surfing the World Wide Web!

## THE EMAIL THANK-YOU NOTE

While email is the least preferred way in which to send a formal thank-you note, it is a wonderful alternative in business, casual, and personal relationships. For example, if your best friend shared her grandmother's secret family recipe or gave you her shoulder to cry on, it would be perfectly fine to send an email thank-you. On the other hand, formality reigns when sending thank-you notes for wedding presents or baby gifts.

Always use your best judgment. If you aren't sure about sending an email thank-you note, don't. Just remember, in today's digital world, handwritten notes are always greatly appreciated. Make an impact and leave a lasting impression.

## PROPER EMAIL FORMATTING

Sending your email thank-you note is easy and differs in format from the ink-and-paper version. Ideally, it should include:

1. **RECIPIENT'S NAME:** Make sure you have the correct email address of the person you are sending your note to. If that person has emailed you before, you should be able to quickly access their contact from your old emails and add it to your address book for future reference.

2. **YOUR NAME:** It is always a good idea to set your name in your email preferences so your recipient can quickly identify the email in their inbox. For example, if your email is GratefulGirl@Karma.com, you would want the recipient's inbox to show your name properly formatted with correct capitalization, like this: Kelly Browne—GratefulGirl@Karma.com.

3. **CC:** If you want to "cc" or "carbon copy" another person on your email and you want your recipient to see who you have copied, then insert their email address here.

4. **BC:** The "blind copy" field should be used on the occasions when you don't want your recipient to see the other name of the person or group you are copying your email to.

5. **SUBJECT:** Include a few words in the subject line so the recipient knows what your email is about. For example, "Thank you for lunch!"

6. **DATE AND TIME:** The date and time stamps are automatically included so there is no need to write it in the body of your note.

7. **BODY:** Include the following in the body of your note:

❈ **SALUTATION**—"Dear" or other terms of endearment are always appreciated, but not always necessary for a casual note. Follow this with the recipient's name and a comma or colon. Use your judgment and consider what is appropriate for each situation. Tip: "Hi (insert name of recipient)," has become a popular casual email greeting. You could write "Hi Louise," for example.

❈ **RECIPIENT'S NAME**—Use the recipient's first name or, when appropriate, use the correct honorific, followed by their first name or surname: "Dear Louise," or "Dear Ms. Cueva," for example. Always check to make sure you have the spelled the recipient's name correctly.

❈ **YOUR NOTE**—Your note should follow the basic spirit of "Writing the Classic Thank-You Note," as outlined in chapter 1. Be sure to keep it brief, use proper grammar, spell-check, check for correct punctuation, and read it over to make sure auto-correct is accurate.

❈ **EMOTICONS AND SMILEY FACES**—These little pictures inserted into your text are always fun to use ☺. While they are perfect for casual notes or text messages, avoid them when you are sending a formal or business note.

❈ **CAPITAL LETTERS AND EXCLAMATION POINTS!**— Since your tone of voice cannot be heard in an email, choose your words to convey your emotion. Do remember that overusing exclamation points and CAPITAL LETTERS can be interpreted as a *flaming* or *screaming text.*

❈ **CLOSING**—To signal the end of your email note, use "Sincerely," "Love," "Cheers," or whatever you feel is suitable for the occasion.

❈ **YOUR NAME**—Always include your name, as it is your *electronic signature.* Depending on the situation or recipient, use your first name, full name, or initials. Do consider setting your *signature stamp* in your email preferences and customizing it to include your closing, name, business address, business logo, or website links.

❋ **ATTACHMENTS**—A picture is worth a thousand words! So are short videos. If you care to share, compress your attachment or use the "insert image" tool so your recipient can feel your appreciation. If you are attaching a document or PDF file, make sure you reference it in the body of your note so the recipient knows to look for it.

Your email should look like this:

*(Automatic date and time stamp)*
**To:** Louise Cueva—RecipientName@Internet.com
**CC:** (insert email address or leave blank if you don't want to copy another recipient)
**BCC:** (insert email address or leave blank if you don't want to blind copy another recipient)
**From:** Kelly Browne—GratefulGirl@Karma.com
**Subject:** Thank You!
Dear Louise,
*(one line space here)*
It was so wonderful to see you today for lunch. Thank you for treating me. Next time, let's go to (name of restaurant), and it will be my turn to treat you!
(one line space here)
During lunch, I mentioned I would send you the link to my page on LinkedIn (insert link here). I would so appreciate any recommendations, leads or ideas you have. Working at (insert name of company) would be my dream job.
Thank you again!
*(one line space here)*
Cheers,
Kelly Browne
(555) 765-4321—mobile
www.KellyBrowne.net

## RESPONDING TO EMAILS

With what feels like hundreds of emails delivered to your inbox each day, quickly sorting through the junk to find the important messages can be time-consuming. By the time you have deleted the spam, you have only glanced at the emails you really need to respond to. If you open an email and read it, sometimes it disappears, then more emails arrive, and suddenly you have forgotten to respond at all. Here are some tips to help you streamline your inbox.

❋ **REPLY IN A TIMELY MANNER**—If someone has taken the time to email you, respond to them within twenty-four hours if possible. While some emails don't require a response, it's always a good idea to acknowledge your receipt so the sender knows you got it. A simple "thank you" reply is sufficient unless it specifies that no reply is necessary.

❋ **REPLY ALL**—When you reply to a group email, you have the option of using "reply" or "reply all." Use discretion when hitting "reply all," as it isn't always necessary to copy everyone on your response.

❋ **FORWARDING AN EMAIL**—If you choose to forward an email, take into consideration the information contained in the possible *chain of emails* that have gone back and forth before you do. Do think twice before forwarding *chain letters,* especially in the workplace.

❋ **FLAG IMPORTANT EMAILS**—If you have only a minute to check your inbox, flag the emails that are a priority so you don't forget to respond, especially if you are checking them on your mobile device.

❋ **CHECK YOUR JUNK MAIL**—Every couple of days, check your junk mail folder to make sure something important didn't accidentally end up in the wrong inbox.

❋ **SEPARATE YOUR EMAIL ACCOUNTS**—Keep your work and personal email accounts separate. Set up another email address to use for things in your life that are not a priority.

❀ **PHISHING EMAIL SCAMS**—Never respond to emails requesting money, personal information, credit cards, bank information, social security numbers, or proclaiming that your password has been compromised. If there is a problem with a password or account, call or log in *directly* to that company's website to verify the change request. Never click through the email.

## SOCIAL MEDIA: PEGGY'S PEARLS OF WISDOM

My mother's pearls of wisdom are timeless and will forever make a difference in promoting global respect on- or off-line. Remember these adages and leave a digital impact!

❀ **"THINK BEFORE YOU SPEAK."**—The same rule applies when you text, email, or post anything online. If you have written something you want to delete, remember that not all social media sites allow you to edit or erase your history. Make sure you know your rights before you write.

❀ **"IF YOU WOULDN'T SAY IT IN PERSON, DON'T SAY IT BEHIND THEIR BACK."**—Hiding behind the virtual armor of a computer screen, people have become more brazen about writing and posting negative comments and profanity online. Don't waste your time; focus on your own life. What you say is a reflection on you.

❀ **"IF YOU HAVE NOTHING NICE TO SAY, DON'T SAY ANYTHING AT ALL!"**—Likewise, if someone posts something mean-spirited about you and you feel it's inappropriate, take a screenshot and report it to the social media company. If you are upset with someone, take a deep breath and don't respond to an email or text in anger—wait, calm down, and think about the best way to handle it. Remember, you can't unsend an email or take back a text, and even if you delete your post, picture, or tweet, someone may already have taken a screenshot on their mobile device or computer without your knowledge, showed it to a friend, forwarded it, or worse, reposted or retweeted it—so THINK before you post!

❊ **"IN JEST, THERE IS TRUTH."** Do remember Shakespeare when you write something, as your words don't always come across in the same spirit as if you were to say them in person. Why? Because your tone of voice can't be heard. Even if you are just "joking around," not everyone may have your sense of humor or want to be publicly teased.

❊ **"PROMISE YOU WON'T TELL ANYONE!"** Don't share the password for your email address; mobile device; social media accounts; or shopping, bank, or credit cards—ever! While you may trust a friend with your deepest secrets in one moment, your friend may not feel the same way about you later on and might be tempted to browse your emails. If you have given out your password, change it immediately to protect yourself and your reputation.

## The Top Fourteen Tips for Cybersecurity

1. **PERSONAL SHIELD**—Protect your legal name and think about using a *nom de plume* or *pseudonym* if you are posting in online forums. If you need to post contact information for yourself, limit it to a nondescript email address and don't use your home address or phone number.

2. **PRIVACY SETTINGS**—Set your spam, content filter, GPS location services, or pop-up windows under "privacy settings" on your computer and mobile devices. You do have the ability to block unwanted emails and text messages.

3. **DOWNLOADS**—Secure your web browser and downloads to protect yourself from unwanted cyber attacks on your system. Review current cybersecurity information and bookmark the United States Computer Emergency Readiness Team at www.us-cert.gov for security tips and cyber threat updates.

4. **FIREWALL**—Make sure your firewall is on to prevent hackers from accessing the personal information on your computer.

5. **SYSTEM UPDATES**—Make sure your antivirus software is up to date and that you have downloaded any available updates for your computer to block hackers from breaking in with malicious code.

6. **ACCESS AND POSTING SETTINGS**—Check your apps to allow/disallow access to your personal information or "push notifications" to your mobile device. If some apps are enabled, they can access your contacts, pictures, and GPS position.

7. **DIGITAL PIRATES**—Even if you think you have your settings private, there will always be an inappropriate email, instant message, attachment, or advertisement you are curious to click on. Try to avoid opening unknown emails, those offering cash rewards, or invitations from digital thieves—who capture your information and sell it for profit.

8. **PASSWORD PROTECTION**—Choose a password that is a combination of uppercase/lowercase letters, numbers, and symbols, and never share it with anyone. If you do, you are giving that person the ability to post information online on your behalf or to send messages to other people in your name. Be smart and keep your details to yourself—then you won't have to worry about it. If your account gets hacked, immediately change your password. It's a good idea to change it regularly.

9. **PURGE**—Make sure you sweep your system regularly by clearing your Internet cache, stored cookies, and any footprints left by companies trying to track your web-browsing history.

10. **DESKTOP CAMERA**—If the green light on your desktop camera is illuminated, remember it's on. To help prevent hackers from spying on your life without your knowledge, cover the camera with a little Post-it®.

11. **COSMIC KARMA**—Don't ever email, text, or post on social media anything negative about someone or any photo that might be harmful to that person's reputation. For one thing, it's inconsiderate and impolite. For another, the consequences of your action might cause a backlash against you. If you have posted something that is considered inappropriate, immediately remove it if you are asked to do so. Remember, if a cyberbully has hurt you, that person's negativity will eventually catch up with them; what goes around comes around.

12. **PROFANITY**—Never use bad language online. Not only do you look foolish, but vulgar as well, and that's the way people will think of you for a long time. If a friend uses profanity on your social media page, simply delete the post. Remember, if you have a public profile, everyone will see it—from family, acquaintances, and friends to business contacts. Be a class act.

13. **BREATHE**—Don't ever send, say, or post threatening messages to anyone, ever! Your action might cause that person to retaliate against you or report you to the authorities. So, if something happens, cool off and do something nice for yourself or someone else.

14. **TURN OFF YOUR COMPUTER**—According to the Federal Bureau of Investigation's website, "With the growth of high-speed Internet connections, many opt to leave their computers on and ready for action. The downside is that being 'always on' renders computers more susceptible. Beyond firewall protection, which is designed to fend off unwanted attacks, *turning the computer off* effectively severs an attacker's connection—be it spyware or a botnet that employs your computer's resources to reach out to other unwitting users." For more tips, visit www.fbi.gov

*How far that little candle throws his beams! So shines a good deed in a naughty world.*

—WILLIAM SHAKESPEARE, *MERCHANT OF VENICE*

# CHAPTER 3

## SOIRÉES AND SOCIAL GATHERINGS

## THANKS FOR HAVING ME

As every gracious young woman knows, cultivating an active social calendar is an important element in creating a successful and fulfilling adult life. Dinner parties, charity events, dances, and social gatherings not only keep you engaged in the rich tapestry of life but often lead to new and exciting relationships and opportunities you never would have encountered had you not been invited. Without the occasional soirée, gala, and reception to look forward to, when would you ever have an excuse to put on that sparkly gown and those completely impractical strappy heels? So the next time you step out in style, let your hosts know what a great time you had by thanking them for inviting you. A grateful guest is a frequent guest.

## WRITING THE SOCIAL THANK-YOU NOTE

1. Remember that all the same basic rules apply to the social or formal thank-you note, so make sure you refer to chapter 1: "Thank-You Notes 101."

2. The use of honorifics is important here, too. If you're sending a thank-you note to your best friend's parents for inviting you to her debutante ball, make sure you use "Mr. and Mrs."

3. Pay attention to your closing as well. A formal honorific requires an elegant closing. "Sincerely" or "Sincerely yours" are more appropriate choices than casual closings such as "With affection."

4. The fold-over informal note or social stationery in white or ecru is always the best choice. Always use black or blue ink when you write the note.

## THE FORMAL SOCIAL ENVELOPE

For formal thank-you notes, the socially correct envelope format is slightly different. The first option is to stagger the lines, with the recipient's name centered on the envelope, followed by the street address underneath and slightly to the right of center, followed by the city, state, and zip code underneath and slightly farther to the right of the address. There should be no abbreviations; everything should be spelled out.

The front of the formal envelope should look like this:

*Mrs. Richard Meldrum Learman*
*1234 Street Place*
*City, State 80000-4321*

Or it can be centered like this:

*Mrs. Richard Meldrum Learman*
*1234 Street Place*
*City, State 80000-4321*

The return address should be printed or written in your best penmanship on the back flap of the envelope. While you can include your formal name, the preferred style is to use only your address. The back flap of the envelope should look like this:

*9000 Avenue Road*
*City, State 10000-1234*

## THE GOLDEN RULES FOR HANDWRITTEN SOCIAL AND SOCIAL MEDIA THANK-YOU SUCCESS

* **MAKE THE PHONE CALL:** Do remember to call your hostess the day after a dinner party you attended the night before, then follow up with a handwritten thank-you note. If you feel it's a casual situation and an email or text would be more appropriate, that's fine, but remember, the personal touch of hearing your voice will always be appreciated.

* **TIMING:** If someone invited you to attend an event or benefit as their guest, be sure to send them a thank-you note within two weeks. A thank-you note would not be expected if you were invited to attend an event and purchased your own ticket.

* **BE PREPARED:** Make sure you always have appropriate stationery on hand to use when necessary so your thank-you note is on time.

* **CHECKING IN ONLINE:** Some occasions become social media check-ins with pictures and hashtags, and guests comment to express their virtual thanks. Celebrate life and be in the moment! Keep your mobile device tucked in your pocketbook. Whatever you decide, remember that saying thank you in a public forum takes away the spirit, intimacy, and elegance of the handwritten note.

❋ **GUEST LIST:** Think before you post a picture at an event or night out for everyone who wasn't included to see. Naturally, not all of your 500+ friends can always make it, but when you post the images of your fabulous soirée, there will be someone who would have liked to have been invited and who will feel left out.

❋ **PICTURES:** Before you post, make sure you get the blessing of the ladies or gentlemen in the picture and that it's flattering to everyone. Sometimes editing the picture with a photo app or adding a filter will improve the candid shot and make everyone look good!

## QUIPS FROM GRATEFUL SAGES THROUGH THE AGES

*For it is in giving that we receive.*

—ST. FRANCIS OF ASSISI

*Carry out a random act of kindness with no expectation of reward, safe in the knowledge that one day someone might do the same for you.*

—DIANA, PRINCESS OF WALES

*Reflect upon your present blessings, of which every man has plenty; not on your past misfortunes, of which all men have some.*

—CHARLES DICKENS, ENGLISH WRITER

*Gratitude is not only the greatest virtue, but the parent of all others.*

—CICERO, ROMAN PHILOSOPHER

*If you knew what I know about the power of giving, you would not let a single meal pass without sharing it in some way.*

—BUDDHA, ENLIGHTENED TEACHER

*I awoke this morning with devout thanksgiving for my friends, the old and the new.*

—RALPH WALDO EMERSON, TRANSCENDENTALIST AUTHOR

## PAY IT FORWARD
### BE AN AMBASSADOR OF GOODWILL

Jacqueline Kennedy Onassis had an incredibly full social calendar, but she presented herself to the world as an ambassador of goodwill with unforgettable grace and dignity. My mother, too, is an example to us all. She has been volunteering her time for as long as I can remember—not just spending countless hours making and serving casseroles at church functions, but even organizing the Angel's Flight Gala to help runaway children. While spearheading paper drives and tennis tournaments, working with National Charity League, and helping the Los Angeles Orphanage Guild, she still finds the time to honor our servicemen and women and the WWII heroes of the Mighty Eighth Air Force with the Heritage League of the Second Air Division. As I watch her in admiration, I also see the utter joy and appreciation on the faces of people whose lives she has directly influenced by her kindness. This has truly affected my life. Honored on both coasts by the mayor of Albany, New York, as a Tulip Princess, *and by the City of Los Angeles* as an Irish Woman of the Year—Honoree for her philanthropy in the community, she has been a light of inspiration to us all and has left an indelible handprint on our hearts.

Perhaps you're thinking you don't have time to work out at the gym, much less volunteer at a soup kitchen. There are things you can do every day to share your appreciation with the world. Donate your old clothes to a battered women's shelter, put your trash in the garbage can, recycle, compost your kitchen scraps, help someone less fortunate than you, make a phone call to help a friend get a job, visit the sick, or give food to a homeless person. My mother always says, "Share your smile; it may be the only positive energy someone sees in a day." Even speaking kindly and respectfully to others is an important contribution. Be an ambassador of goodwill, and people will remember you.

## THANKS FOR HAVING ME
## —SAMPLE NOTES

It is essential to send a thank-you note for each event you have been invited to as a guest. Whether it be for a dinner, a weekend at someone's home, or a charity event, a note of thanks must be sent. On the following pages are some sample thank-you notes you can copy, fill in, or use for inspiration as you write your own.

### THANKS FOR THE DINNER OR DINNER PARTY

Dear _____,

*I just want to thank you again for the delicious dinner at your gorgeous home last evening. I so appreciate your attention to every detail and the love you put into everything you do. Please know I will remember this special night for a long time to come.*

*Sincerely yours,*

_____

My dear _____,

*In the words of Shakespeare, "Small cheer and great welcome makes a merry feast." Dinner was divine and the company even more exquisite. I so appreciate your graciousness and simply cannot wait to return.*

*A thousand thank-yous,*

_____

Dear _____,

*Nothing is more wonderful than breaking bread with the people you love and toasting to life. The wine, amazing food, and stimulating conversation created memories we will forever cherish. Here's to many more priceless moments! Thank you, thank you, thank you!*

*Love,*

_____

THANKS FOR HOSTING THE POTLUCK PARTY

Dear _____,

What a wonderful idea to throw a dinner party and have everyone bring their favorite dish! It made the night so entertaining, and we felt proud to share our much-loved recipes with our friends. Thank you for bringing us together and creating a memorable evening.

Yours truly,

_____

THANKS FOR THE FABULOUS AFFAIR OR GALA
FOR AN EVENT, COMPANY, OR CHARITY

Dear _____,

The (name of event) was utterly spectacular! Thank you for including me in your elegant affair, which has definitely spoiled me forever. I wish you my heartfelt congratulations on the success of (name of event, company, charity) and offer my sincere appreciation to you for inviting me as your guest. It was truly a magical night.

Most sincerely,

_____

Dear _____,

The (name of event, tea party, luncheon, etc.) for (name of charity) was truly an event I will never forget. I deeply appreciated your inviting me to attend and allowing me the opportunity to see firsthand the work that is being done for this deserving cause. Please include me on the guest list for next year's fundraiser. Thank you again for such a moving day that left handprints on my heart.

Sincerely,

_____

## THANK YOU FOR THE EXHIBIT, CONCERT, OR SHOW

Dear _____,

I know that the tickets for (name of event) were sold out and difficult to get. I was simply thrilled when you (called or emailed) and (gave me your tickets or invited me to attend with you). Please know it was truly an experience I will never forget. Thank you for such a wonderful treat and the opportunity to enjoy this amazing night.

Sincerely yours,

_____

## THANK YOU, MR. AMBASSADOR, FOR INVITING ME TO THE RECEPTION

Dear Mr. Ambassador,

What a pleasure it was to make your acquaintance last evening at the (name of event) reception for (person's name). I truly admire the work you have done, and I hope our lawmakers look to your ideas to promote peace. If there is anything I can do to support your mission, please let me know. Thank you for including me in this unforgettable night.

Respectfully yours,

_____

### GRATEFUL SAGE TIP

If you are responding to an online invitation via sites like www.evite.com or www.paperlesspost. com, try to do so within a few days of receiving the invitation so your host can plan accordingly.

## THANK YOU FOR THE WEEKEND AWAY

*Dear _____,*

*My weekend at your home in (name of location) was simply magical. I
can still smell the delicious (BBQ/dinner/breakfast/lunch) we had and
taste that amazing (name of dessert or wine, etc.) How did the two of you
become such incredible gourmet chefs? Please know I appreciated that you
made me feel so welcome in every way. I look forward to seeing you both
again soon.*

*Sincerely yours,*

_____

## THANK YOU FOR THE INVITATION—
## ACCEPT OR REGRET

If you are sending an email response, you could send something
casual like this:

*Dear Mr. and Mrs. _____,*

*I accept with pleasure your kind invitation to attend the celebration for
(name of person)'s birthday on (day and date) at the (name of location) at
(time of day). Thank you for including me in the festivities!*

*Most sincerely,*

_____

*Dear_____,*

*Thank you for the kind invitation to your party. Unfortunately, I am
already committed for that evening and will be unable to attend. I
appreciate your thinking of me and know it will be a great success. Please
keep me on your list for the next time.*

*Sincerely yours,*

_____

*Words have the power to both destroy and heal. When words are both true and kind, they can change our world.*

—BUDDHA, ENLIGHTENED TEACHER

# CHAPTER 4

## PERSONAL MILESTONES AND SPECIAL MOMENTS

## THANKS FOR THE WONDERFUL MEMORIES

Whether you're graduating, celebrating a birthday, moving into a new home, marking a personal achievement, attending your first ball, or embarking on your next global tour, the good wishes—and, of course, the many thoughtful gifts from family and friends—make those remarkable moments in life truly special, creating memories that will last a lifetime. So the next time you reach a personal milestone, take a moment to let people know just how much their love and generosity mean to you.

### GRATEFUL SAGE TIPS

* If you don't know what to give the person who seems to have everything, think about making a financial contribution in that person's name to a favorite charity.

* Even if you thanked someone enthusiastically when you opened the gift, you must still send a thank-you note.

* Make your note personal and conversational; write it as if you were speaking with the person who gave you the gift.

### Sparkling Birthstones

These legendary gemstones make fabulous birthday gifts!

| | |
|---|---|
| January | Garnet |
| February | Amethyst |
| March | Aquamarine, bloodstone |
| April | Diamond (great for all occasions!) |
| May | Emerald |
| June | Pearl, moonstone, alexandrite |
| July | Ruby |
| August | Peridot, sardonyx |
| September | Sapphire |
| October | Opal, tourmaline |
| November | Topaz, citrine |
| December | Turquoise, zircon |

### Birthday Netiquette

❋ Sending a digital thank-you note? Handwritten is *always* best, but if you want to use your computer or mobile device, check out thank-you apps. Some stationery apps like www. RedStamp.com will allow you to write your note, upload a photo, access your contacts, and email, share, or—better yet— mail your thank-you as a postcard or note in an envelope for a small fee through the U.S. Postal Service.

❋ Do think twice *before* posting a picture of your birthday party on social media websites if you think someone's feelings might be hurt. If you do, make sure the picture you post is appropriate and won't embarrass anyone.

❋ Never, *ever* thank someone for a birthday gift on social media sites *instead of* sending a thank-you note—it's tacky and impersonal.

❋ Avoid using a text message to thank someone for a gift. If you want to let your friend know you got their gift and share your excitement, great, go ahead, but you still need to send a note of thanks.

## PAY IT FORWARD
### BIRTHDAY GRATITUDE IN ACTION

A great way to say thank you to your friends and family for their help in making your life extraordinary is to remember their birthdays and significant events. It's the little things, like simply being thought of, that create a sudden burst of magic by lighting up someone's day.

❋ PAPER BIRTHDAY CALENDAR: Do an Internet search for a "PDF birthday calendar" and download one for free. Enter all the birthday or anniversary dates you need to remember, creating a master list so you can easily refer to it for years to come.

❋ ONLINE ADDRESS BOOK: Most virtual address book apps have a "birthday" field on each "contact card," allowing you to input a birthday or anniversary and sync the card to your calendar app so the info appears in your schedule.

❋ VIRTUAL CALENDAR: Look at the calendar app your computer uses and input your important dates to remember with a reminder alert. You should only need to set it once as a perpetual prompt.

❋ DIGITAL GREETING: Some greeting card websites will allow you to create e-cards in advance. They can then be sent on a specified date, so if you're traveling and can't send your best friend an e-card on her special day, no need to worry—the website will send it for you! Or the event alarm might just propel you to send a real card through the mail!

❋ SOCIAL MEDIA: If you allow access to your contacts and calendar, social media sites like Facebook will sync your friends' birthdays to your calendars with reminder alerts and invitations to send virtual gifts. Tip: Do be cautious when allowing any app to have access to your personal information.

❋ E-GIFTS: Most companies today allow you to purchase electronic gift cards online with the option of sending them via email, the postal service, or overnight express delivery.

❖ VIDEO CHAT: Sometimes the best way to say happy birthday is in person! But if you can't be there, why not send your love and best wishes via video chat?

❖ BUY BIRTHDAY CARDS IN ADVANCE: If you see a birthday card you love, buy it. It's always a good idea to have a supply of a few fabulous birthday cards on hand.

## THANKS FOR THE WONDERFUL MEMORIES—SAMPLE NOTES

Here are some sample notes to help you say thanks for the memories with elegance and impact.

THANK YOU FOR MY BIRTHDAY GIFT

Dear _____,

How very thoughtful of you to think of me on my birthday. I just love the (gift) and want you to know that every time I (wear it, see it, use it), I think of you. Thank you for all your generosity. I look forward to seeing you soon. With all my love,

_____

Dear _____,

The (gift) you gave me for my birthday is perfect! I love it! I know you put so much thought into finding something amazing, and that means the world to me. Thank you for making me feel so special! With much love to you,

_____

*Dear _____,*

*Thank you for making my birthday unforgettable! I adore the (gift) you gave me and will treasure it always. Thank you so very much for helping me celebrate another fabulous year!*

*Cheers,*

_____

*Dear_____,*

*Wow! What can I say but thank you from the bottom of my heart for the most amazing gift ever! I love the (gift) so much and look forward to (using it, reading it, spending it, etc.) A million thanks!*

*Hugs,*

_____

*Dear _____,*

*Oh my gosh! I love it! How do you always find me the perfect gift? I am so grateful for your thoughtfulness and for having you in my life. I adore you!*

*Love,*

_____

## THANK YOU FOR THE BEST FRIEND SPA DAY BIRTHDAY

*Dear _____,*

*Oh my goodness, I had the most amazing time! Thank you for spending the day with me at the spa and celebrating my birthday. More important, I am so grateful for the gift of your love and friendship, which means the world to me. Thank you for making this day something I will treasure for a lifetime.*

*Lots of love,*

_____

*Dear _____,*

*Oh, you got me! I am still shocked! I thought everyone was acting strange, but I never imagined I was walking into my own surprise party. Please know it meant so much to me that you went to such great lengths to make sure I had a special celebration for my birthday. I will never forget your love and kindness—thank you from the bottom of my heart.*

*Gratefully yours,*

_____

*Dear Mom and Dad,*

*There are simply no words to express how deeply I appreciate your helping me buy a (car/something fabulous)! I never imagined that (on my birthday/graduation/just because) my dream would come true. I know you have both worked so hard to give me this, and in return, I want you to know that I will continue to focus on my (schoolwork/career/other efforts). Thank you for believing in me and having confidence in my ability to make good decisions.*

*With all my love, always,*

_____

## BON VOYAGE—MOVING TO COLLEGE, SEMESTER AWAY

*Dear _____,*

*I can't tell you how much I appreciated your being at my bon voyage party to help send me off. I am really looking forward to going to (name of country/name of college), but I will miss you desperately. I love the (gift cards/headset for video chatting) and promise to post pictures of my adventures. While my departure is bittersweet, thank you for making it très magnifique! Au revoir, mon amie!*

*Merci,*

_____

## THANKS FOR COMING TO MY DEBUTANTE CHARITY BALL

*Dear _____,*

*It was such an honor to have you at my debutante ball last Saturday evening to celebrate all the young ladies and our philanthropic efforts in the community. Your presence was a gift in itself, but please know I so appreciated your donation in support of (favorite charity). Thank you for sharing this unforgettable evening with me and joining me in the effort to make a difference in our world.*

*My sincere thanks,*

_____

---

---

*Dear Professor _____,*

*I can't believe that the moment I have worked so hard for has finally arrived. While I am excited to graduate and move on to the next chapter of my life, it is also bittersweet. You have influenced my life decisions, broadened my horizons, and encouraged me to reach farther than I ever dreamed I could. Thank you for making a difference and leaving your indelible handprint on my heart.*

*Most sincerely,*

_____

---

---

*Dear _____,*

*It meant so much to me to have you at my graduation. Looking out into the audience and seeing you cheering as I received my diploma was a moment I will forever cherish. From my heart, I thank you for sharing this personal achievement with me and encouraging me to challenge myself. Thank you for believing I could do it.*

*With affection,*

_____

## GRATEFUL SAGE TIP

Remember, even if you send out or receive a graduation announcement card, a gift isn't required in return.

### GRATEFUL SAGE TIP

Celebrate your successes on social media! Here's a wonderful opportunity to announce your degree and inspire others to achieve their dreams!

THANKS FOR THE FABULOUS GRADUATION GIFT—
WISH YOU WERE HERE!

Dear _____,

It was so generous of you to send me a check for my graduation from (name of school). Although I wished you were here, I knew that all your good wishes were with me. I so appreciate the (gift card/check) you sent and I plan on (putting it to good use/using it to pay off my student loans/getting a new computer/buying a suit for my first job interview). Let's celebrate the next time we're together. Thank you for your thoughtfulness.

Lots of love,

_____

THANKS, MOM AND DAD, FOR COLLEGE

Dear Mom and Dad,

What can I say but thank you, thank you, thank you—for always supporting me along my journey of life and insisting that the foundation be a good education. Thank you for never letting me quit, for believing that I could do anything, and giving me the tools to help me leave my mark on this world. Yes, I did it—but I couldn't have done it without your support. I love you both and am forever grateful.

With all my love,

_____

## THANK YOU FOR WARMING MY NEW HOME WITH YOUR LOVE AND GOOD WISHES

*Dear _____,*

*No way could I ever have moved into my new apartment without your help!
Thank you for helping me pack, carry boxes, bags, and everything in between,
and for doing it in such good spirits. I would love to have you back for dinner
to show my appreciation, so please let me know when you have a free night in
the coming weeks. Thank you!*

*Gratefully yours,*

_____

*Dear _____,*

*Thank you so much for helping me celebrate my new home and coming to
my housewarming party. I loved all of the amazing recipes you shared and
simply cannot wait to make them! Now that I have a place to call my own, I
will definitely be spending time in the kitchen developing my culinary skills!
Thanks again!*

*Love,*

_____

## THANKS FOR THE DONATION TO MY CHARITY FUNDRAISER

*Dear _____,*

*It is with my profound appreciation that I thank you from the bottom of
my heart for your generous contribution to (name of your favorite charity).
Your donation will not only change lives but allow this important work to
carry on in our community and inspire others to make a difference. It is these
random acts of kindness, big or small, that effect change and promote a spirit
of goodwill worldwide. Thank you!*

*My sincerest gratitude,*

_____

GRATEFUL SAGE TIP

The next time someone asks you for gift ideas,
request personalized stationery; then send
that person a thank-you note on it!

## The Blessings List

Nothing is more powerful than counting your blessings and being grateful for what you have in this world. Did you know jealously is the absence of gratitude? It's true. Make a list of what you are grateful for or visit www.KellyBrowne.net and download The Blessings List. Any time you're feeling blue, take out this list and write one more thing you feel appreciation for. As you remember the food on your table, to your parents, friends, health, or the roof over your head, this list can change your life.

### QUIPS FROM GRACIOUS AND SPECIAL SAGES THROUGH THE AGES

*Thousands of candles can be lit from a single candle, and the life of the candle will not be shortened. Happiness never decreases by being shared.*

—BUDDHA, ENLIGHTENED TEACHER

*No act of kindness, no matter how small, is ever wasted.*

—AESOP, GREEK STORYTELLER

*If the only prayer you ever say in your whole life is "thank you," that would suffice.*

—MEISTER ECKHART, GERMAN PHILOSOPHER

*Forget injuries, never forget kindnesses.*

—CONFUCIUS, CHINESE PHILOSOPHER

"*Your time is limited, so don't waste it living someone else's life. Don't be trapped by dogma—which is living with the results of other people's thinking. Don't let the noise of others' opinions drown out your own inner voice. And most important, have the courage to follow your heart and intuition. They somehow already know what you truly want to become. Everything else is secondary.*"

—STEVE JOBS, COFOUNDER, APPLE COMPUTERS,
STANFORD UNIVERSITY COMMENCEMENT SPEECH,
JUNE 2005

# CHAPTER 5
## CLIMBING THE LADDER OF SUCCESS

## THANKS FOR THE OPPORTUNITY

The ability to write a gracious and memorable thank-you note has advantages that extend far beyond the social world and can actually make a huge difference in getting your dream job or creating your golden opportunity. Writing a thank-you note following a job interview not only shows the interviewer that you have good, professional manners; it also helps you stand out from the crowd of other candidates. Even if you don't get the job, sending a good-natured thank-you note reiterating your interest can turn rejection into a new possibility for success, should the situation change. Like everything else, business involves maintaining good relationships with the people you meet along the way and making sure they realize how appreciative you are for any help they can offer. If you don't personally thank someone who helped you, chances are they won't help you again. So the next time you're planning to take a step up the ladder of success, remember to look behind you and thank the people who gave you a break or put in a good word for you. They will appreciate it, and you will, too, when you land the job of your dreams!

*There is always room at the top*

—DANIEL WEBSTER,
AMERICAN ORATOR AND STATESMAN

## When to Send the Business Thank-You Note

❋ Send a handwritten or computer-generated thank-you note immediately following a job interview and no later than two days afterward if you are emailing it. An immediate follow-up to your meeting shows you would make a conscientious and productive employee, executive, consultant, or vendor.

❋ Send a note to any person who spoke on your behalf, referred you for a position, or wrote a letter of recommendation for you.

❋ If you don't get the job, send a thank-you note reiterating your interest should a position become available later.

❋ If company circumstances change and the job is no longer available, thank your contacts for taking the time to speak with you and ask if they'll pass along your résumé.

❋ Send thank-you notes when people do something thoughtful for you such as referring business, taking you to lunch or dinner, sending you a gift, or giving you tickets to an event.

❋ Business owners should always take the time to thank their customers for their continued loyalty.

❋ If you're leaving your current position, it is gracious to include a personal note of thanks along with your letter of resignation.

### GRATEFUL SAGE TIP

A traditional way to thank a client or friend in a small but polite way is to take the person out for a cup of coffee. Coffee gift cards are an affordable alternative and an excellent idea to include with your thank-you note. Think creatively!

## THE BUSINESS THANK-YOU NOTE— THE BASICS

The business thank-you note opens the door for further communication and gives you the ability to add one more point to your interview. Use this opportunity as your final selling tool and to reiterate your desire to work there. There's no need to restate your résumé, but do use this note to express any additional ideas you might have or to add something you forgot to say in the interview. How well you write this note will reflect how you represent yourself and the how you would represent the company. More important, you are demonstrating that you are not only smart but also a person with excellent values and social grace.

* Do keep your note concise and limited to one page. Always be sincere and professional in what you write. Know your audience and maintain the appropriate level of formality in your salutation and closing.

* Do use your creativity and design a professional-looking letterhead or, if starting your own business, have a good logo designed that is consistent with your brand and embodies your values.

* Don't make the mistake of forgetting to change the interviewer's name in the address and "Dear" sections if you are sending out more than one thank-you note that's been created on your computer or with mail-merge tools. Also double check that you have the correct spelling of the person's name in your letter. Would you hire someone who spelled your name wrong in a thank-you note?

* Do proofread your letter. Always read it out loud and use the spell-check option in your word-processing or email program. Check for punctuation and proper capitalization. You can lose a job simply because you were sloppy.

❋ Do use black or blue ink for handwritten notes and follow the format guidelines in chapter 1: "Thank-You Notes 101."

❋ Do handwrite your signature in black or blue ink for computer-generated notes.

❋ Do reiterate your desire for the position, clarify any uncertainties the interviewer might have expressed, and show your strengths. Say, "I will follow up with you next week." Ask for the sale!

A professional letter, the business thank-you note includes proper spacing, the date, and company contact information, as well as your personal contact information.

It should look like this:

*April 26, 2016* (*date at the top of the page*)

(four line spaces between the date and person's name)
*Ms. Margaret Learman*
*St. George Media*
*4320 West 42nd Street*
*New York, NY 10019*
(two line spaces between the last address line and your salutation)
*Dear Ms. Learman:* (use a colon here instead of a comma)
(one line space here)

*I wanted to take a moment to thank you for meeting with me this afternoon. I am well aware of the pressure and excitement that accompany working at (name of company), and I appreciate the generous time you took to look at my work. Although I am a recent graduate of (insert name) design school, I have spent many hours interning with several companies and have attached their recommendations for your review.*
(one line space between paragraphs)

*While I am aware that this week is hectic for you, I wanted to let you know that should a position become available I would be thrilled to join your team. I am attaching a color copy of one of my designs for your reference.*

(one line space)

*Thank you again for taking the time to meet me.*

(one line space)

*Sincerely,*

(four line spaces—to handwrite your name)

*Kelly Browne*

*mobile number*

*website address link for your online portfolio*

*social media links*

## Global Gratitude Business Tips

With the evolution of globalization, protocol has become a highly sophisticated and strategic asset in today's business, military, and diplomatic world. Keep in mind these leadership tips from Pamela Eyring, president of The Protocol School of Washington®, for supporting international relations and being a universal role model.

❋ Self-awareness of one's professional behavior is critical when building relationships at work.

❋ Always treat everyone with respect and pay attention to how someone treats others; it's a true indicator of how they will treat you.

❋ When building your business relationships around the world, make sure to do in-depth research on the customs and business protocol specific to the countries you are working in.

❋ Remember the pearls your mother taught you: eye contact, the firm handshake, and *please* and *thank you* go a long way toward promoting civility and mutual respect.

❋ For more information and training, please visit www.psow.edu.

## The Business Stationery Checklist

❀ Use paper that is a higher quality than regular white copy paper.

❀ Standard business-size 8½″ x 11″ sheets are available in watermarked, 100 percent cotton paper in ecru or white. Stay away from colors.

❀ Monarch sheets or executive sheets are smaller and available in 7¼″ x 10½″ size. These are perfect for the personal business note and fit easily through a printer if necessary.

❀ The business correspondence card size is 4½″ x 6½″ and is a heavier card stock. These cards are used for occasions that are professional but a bit more personal.

❀ Do order customized letterhead with your name and address or create your own on the computer. Always use a matching envelope that includes your return address.

❀ For security today, some women eliminate their home address from their résumé and use only their mobile phone number and email address as a contact. This is a good point to consider if you post your résumé with a headhunter or on job-resource websites.

❀ Office supply stores carry Crane & Co. letter-size business paper with matching envelopes for your thank-you notes, correspondence, cover letter, and résumé. Visit www. Crane.com to view the online selections.

## Fourteen Things Every Grateful Interviewee Should Know

1. Research the company before the interview so you know enough about it to show your interest, speak intelligently, and ask informed questions.

2. Bring an extra copy of your résumé to leave on the interviewer's desk so they have it easily accessible and to show you are prepared for the meeting.

3. Include a small professional picture of yourself on your résumé, especially if your interviewer is meeting with dozens of candidates. It will help them to remember you.

4. Dress appropriately for the position and always arrive early. Polished shoes and fresh clean clothes are a must.

5. Shake your interviewer's hand firmly when you meet her, look her in the eye, and thank her for the opportunity to interview. Make sure you say thank you again when you leave.

6. Get your interviewer's business card with her email and business address. Then you can be sure all your information is correct, and it's an easy way to follow up later.

7. Always get the name of the assistant who helps you or sets up a meeting for you. Make sure to thank them, either in person or by sending a follow-up email. Assistants are truly the portal guardians, and being kind and gracious to them really helps to ensure your access. Remember, that assistant just might become the CEO of the company one day.

8. Look around your interviewer's office and note something unique in the surroundings. It will help you make a personal connection in your thank-you note and will show you were paying attention. This is especially perfect if you are interviewing for marketing, sales, or ad agency jobs and will provide an opportunity to demonstrate your creative expertise.

9. Your interviewer will look at your educational background. In today's competitive job market, having a degree is vital to your success. It helps you to stand out and move toward the CEO position. If you want that dream job you've wished for your whole life, you have to work hard to attain it.

10. If you need experience to get the job you want, consider doing volunteer work or working as an intern. Ask for a

record of your community service or letter of reference. These are easy ways for you to start a résumé even when you are still in high school or college, or looking for a job.

11. Make sure your online professional network page is up to date and that you have good references. If you are uploading an image of yourself, have a professional photographer take a picture of you if you can.

12. It's likely that your interviewer will do an Internet search on you before you arrive to ascertain your public image online. Remember, social media sites are public bulletin boards and what you post is not private.

13. Set up a professional website that your job interviewer can look at. There are several online website service companies that allow you to set up a free site or charge a nominal fee to display your photography talents, media technical savvy, or blogging, or to showcase videos of your expertise. Think outside the box and show the world what you can do.

14. Secure your education and get your degree. It does make a difference in getting the job you want and working your way up the ladder of success. Take one class at a time, check out your options online, or contact your local community college or university to find out about evening and weekend programs.

## VIRTUAL GRATITUDE: THE FUNDAMENTALS OF THANK-YOU NOTE NETIQUETTE

Many corporations today prefer using email for the majority of their business. It makes sense, then, that many companies readily accept this form of a thank-you note for interviews, meetings, business lunches, and dinners because it is efficient, cost effective, professional, instantaneous, and gives you access to someone you might not have had contact with otherwise. Whether or not you send an email thank-you note is really a matter of discretion, so use your best judgment. The advantage of email is that it is immediately received by your interviewer.

## THE SUCCESSFUL EMAIL BUSINESS THANK-YOU NOTE CHECKLIST

In addition to following the basic rules of writing the business note, an email thank-you to your interviewer must look professional, be well thought out, and avoid the use of acronyms, emoticons, and slang. For example, don't write acronyms like "TY" for thank you or use emoticons like ☺.

* ❄ Don't run home and send your emailed thank-you note right away. You just left. Wait a few hours. The objective is to remind them of you.

* ❄ Keep in mind that your thank-you note could be caught by a spam filter and never arrive, so make sure you include a few words in your subject line like "Thank You for the Interview." Verify the email address before you send it.

* ❄ Maintain a professional email address. You don't want to lose a job opportunity because your interviewer feels your email address is inappropriate. Using your name, initials, or a combination thereof is always a good option. If your choice isn't available, try using a number at the end of your name, like this example: KellyBrowne6@Internet.com

## PROPER EMAIL FORMAT FOR BUSINESS THANK-YOUS

The format of an emailed thank-you note is really a blend of the handwritten and the business notes. Because the addressee's email is already included, there's no need to rewrite it in the body of the message.

Typically, the email thank-you includes your salutation, followed by the person's name, your thank-you message, the closing, and your name, followed by your contact information. It should look like this:

**To:** Frank.Learman@consolidated.com
**From:** EstherMeldrum@Internet.net
**Date:** 2-15-2016 9:00AM PST
**Subject:** Thank You

Dear Mr. Learman:

I just want to follow up and let you know how much I appreciated meeting with you today. It would be such an honor for me to work at Consolidated and participate in the development of cutting-edge aerospace technology. Should a position become open in your Research and Development department, please let me know.

Thank you again for taking the time to meet with me.

Sincerely,

Esther Meldrum
(415) 555-1212—mobile
(415) 555-1313—home
450 Center Drive
San Francisco, CA 90005-1234

---

GRATEFUL SAGE TIP

Life is too short to stay in a job you don't enjoy. Challenge yourself, have imagination, and create your own magic.

When in doubt about which type of thank-you to use, choose the computer-generated or emailed thank-you note because they are the most common formats in the business world.

## QUIPS FROM PRESIDENTIAL SAGES THROUGH THE AGES

*In writing or speaking, give to every person his due title according to his degree and custom of the place.*

—GEORGE WASHINGTON

*I never considered a difference of opinion in politics, in religion, in philosophy, as cause for withdrawing from a friend.*

—THOMAS JEFFERSON

*Common sense and consideration should be the basis of etiquette and good manners.*

—JOHN QUINCY ADAMS

*As we express our gratitude, we must never forget that the highest appreciation is not to utter words, but to live by them.*

—JOHN FITZGERALD KENNEDY

*Gratitude is a way to a deeper wisdom. Look for the deeper wisdom; believe me, there's a great hunger for it. And here you're in luck. As Americans, you have a special claim to it.*

—RONALD REAGAN

## WHEN YOU LAND YOUR DREAM JOB—
## DIGITAL TIPS TO REMEMBER

* **V-CARD**: Create an *electronic business card* to include with your email correspondence, website, or text messages. It will allow your business associates and clients to download your information and immediately import it into their contacts. Include your company logo, picture, video link, and social media links to make it easy for them to contact you.

* **PERSONAL EMAILS**: Avoid using your business email address for personal use. If you don't have a personal email address, you can set up a free Gmail account at Google.com or with Apple via iCloud.com, among others. These services have varying features and tools; do your online research to decide what Internet service works best for you.

* **CLARIFYING A MEETING OR CONVERSATION**: Do use email to reiterate the points of a meeting or conversation for clarity. Keep it concise and break it out into bullet points so it's easy to read.

* **INAPPROPRIATE EMAILS**: Never forward an inappropriate email. You don't want to get caught up in the distribution of something that's inappropriate, should a problem arise.

* **ATTACHING FILES**: When sending a file via email, be sure to mention the attachment in your note so the recipient will know to look for it. For large files consider uploading to website file-sharing services like Dropbox, MediaFire, 4Shared, and others.

* **REDUCING FILE ATTACHMENTS**: Use the "reduce your file size" tool to quickly send pictures, graphics, documents, and PDF files. If your attachment is too large, your email may not go through. For sharing pictures, consider using mobile apps like Shutterfly, Snapfish, Dropbox, or Flickr.

❈ **FORWARDING EMAILS**: If you forward on an email to someone with information that was not intended for the person you are sending it to, you might violate your company's privacy laws. Think twice before you press "send."

❈ **SUBJECT**: Start a new email if the intended content of your subject is a new matter.

❈ **CANCELING A LUNCH OR A MEETING**: If you are canceling a lunch or appointment days in advance, offer the recipient other possible days when you can reschedule. If you are canceling the day of, always make sure the person received your email, or call to confirm.

❈ **RELIGIOUS AND POLITICAL EMAILS**: Be smart and keep your point of view to yourself. Never forward political or religious emails within your office or business. Not everyone shares your opinion, and you might offend someone without even realizing it, which could compromise your effectiveness at your job and jeopardize your livelihood—and perhaps your employer's.

❈ **AUTOMATIC REPLY**: Set your automatic reply to confirm receipt of emails and offer other contact alternatives if you are going to be away from the office and unable to respond to your emails in a timely manner.

❈ **SOCIAL MEDIA**: Really think twice about being friends with your business supervisor on social media. It's always better to keep your personal details private.

❈ **DISCLAIMER**: If you own a company and want to help protect yourself from or discourage the dissemination of private information, consult an attorney for a proper disclaimer to add at the bottom of your email regarding copyright infringement, privacy, viruses, expressed views, and other issues.

❋ **NEGATIVE NEWS**: Anytime you are delivering bad news or terminating an employee, always do it in person—never by email. Remember that losing a job is a deeply personal situation that can profoundly affect someone's life and livelihood. The delivery of the message requires politeness and sensitivity, which is better communicated with personal contact.

## PAY IT FORWARD

### VOLUNTEERING FOR SUCCESS

Volunteer work is critical to your success and has an enormous positive effect on your résumé. It not only presents you as someone who is willing to give back to your community without expecting anything in return, but sets you apart from the other job candidates. My mother encouraged my participation in National Charity League, Inc.—San Fernando Valley Chapter, a philanthropic mother-daughter debutante program that embraces volunteer service in the community. As part of my service, I worked for years with the Crippled Children Society, now known as AbilityFirst. I stuffed envelopes, collected money, and worked with special-needs children to earn my volunteer hours. In college, my sorority, Delta Delta Delta, continued the spirit of giving back. I didn't know it at the time, but it changed me forever. I learned to be patient, compassionate, thankful, and nonjudgmental. I began to look at the world in a different way, and it made me the woman I am today. After a while, I realized that the things that I deeply valued in my life didn't have a price tag on them. As I entered the workforce and applied for my first job, the interviewer was so impressed that I had spent a significant amount of time in high school and college helping other people and giving back to my community that I was hired on the spot. Volunteering isn't about giving up your summer or even your whole life to join the Peace Corps. Helping to raise money for a cause or participating in an act of charity not only puts community service on your résumé, but makes you feel good. Such experiences will definitely change your life and can provide experience in your chosen field of employment. Even business owners benefit when they participate in local and national campaigns to raise awareness for a charitable cause. Their businesses get exposure, customers feel they're contributing, and as a result, repeat business is likely. The bottom line is—everybody wins.

**GRATEFUL SAGE TIP**
Remember, you aren't born with good manners
and social graces, you must learn them.

## THE HISTORY OF MS.

According to etiquette expert Dorothea Johnson, author and founder of The Protocol School of Washington®, "Ms." is the correct honorific for a woman in the business arena, regardless of what she chooses to call herself in her private life. Revived by twentieth-century feminists, "Ms." has been around since at least the seventeenth century as an abbreviation for the honorific "Mistress," which applied to both married and unmarried women, and from which both "Miss" and "Mrs." derive.

## BUSINESS OWNERS: THANK YOU FOR YOUR CONTINUED LOYALTY

Whether your business is enormous or consists of a small group of clients, the fact remains that your customers appreciate being thanked for their continued loyalty. With our increasing reliance on technology, the personal touch can make all the difference in the growth and success of your business. Thanking your clients can promote a deeper sense of loyalty to you, increase business, and help secure referrals. Equally important is thanking the people who work for you. You will benefit when you thank them for their work and dedication. After all, they are contributing to your success. It's also important for you to model the kind of behavior you would like your staff to project. If you give the gift of gratitude, you will receive it in return.

In this arena, there are limitless ways to show your appreciation:

❈ Provide your employees with thank-you cards so they can send handwritten notes to all their best customers. The personal touch will help you stand out from your competitors. Remember, not everyone is online, so always include your business card with your note.

❈ For the holidays or "just because," send important clients gift baskets, bottles of wine, or gift cards.

❈ Unite your team and host a lunch to publicly recognize a good quality of each of your associates and express how much you appreciate their time and energy. A small token of your gratitude can help keep spirits high and your employees happy. Remember, they represent your brand to the world.

❈ Always personally thank every single person who works for you. Everyone's job is integral to your success, and it's important for each person to feel acknowledged. Whether on their birthday or at the end of the year, many employees hope for a gift or bonus that shows your appreciation for their efforts.

### Five Ways to Promote Your Business in a Virtual World

1. WEBSITES—Your website is your virtual front door, and how it looks will dictate whether possible patrons will want to click through and browse your merchandise. Invest in a site that looks professional and allows easy access so you can update it when necessary. Make sure your site is an efficient go-to portal to link to your services and valuable promotional materials like your blog, pictures, video clips, streaming video, media links, and events. Do an Internet search for the current

best website domain services and builders, and compare their varying costs, available tools, and templates to set up a site that will work for you. Some are completely free.

2. **APPS**—Apps are another opportunity to provide a digital avenue to bring traffic to your website and give you the unique ability to provide a virtual parking spot on a mobile device. Consider setting up features like "push notifications" that allow direct marketing alerts to mobile devices, access to contacts, and the convenience of sharing praise by linking to social media sites.

3. **NEWSLETTERS, BLOGS, AND EMAILS**—Connecting to your customers and reminding them of you is essential in today's competitive marketplace. A blog allows you to create and control your own brand content. A blog can then be easily posted on your website or emailed as a newsletter to your customer database, giving you the unique opportunity to share ideas and endorse your business. Make sure to include a "Sign Up for Our Newsletter" field on your site so your customers can easily subscribe. Browse the competitive newsletter services that offer effortless design templates allowing you to easily drop in your graphics and insert your text.

4. **SOCIAL MEDIA PROFILES**—Take a look at how you can interact with your customers; retweet their praise or posts about your business to encourage your online presence in the marketplace. Facebook, Twitter, Instagram, Pinterest, Yelp, and YouTube, among other social media apps, are essential marketing tools in business, as they allow your customers to access information about your services or products online and share, check reviews, or to compare your business to another. Some of these apps will also allow you to pay for advertisements and access a larger potential clientele.

5. **ONLINE INCENTIVES**—Show your customers your gratitude with online incentives like gift cards, a percentage off services, or coupons to thank them for their business, or for shopping

with you, "checking in" at, or "liking" your store. Make sure your designated #hashtags are clearly visible on your website with your social media links.

## GRATEFUL SAGE TIP

Advertisers use *product placement* to flash brands and products across motion picture and television screens, which often causes a surge in consumer purchasing. Offer your own incentives to patrons when they snap pics or videos and post them to your social media page, or mark them with your #hashtag to show how customers use your brand.

# THANKS FOR THE OPPORTUNITY—
# SAMPLE NOTES

Customize any of these thank-you notes to suit your personal needs!

### THANK YOU FOR THE BUSINESS INTERVIEW

*Dear Ms. _____:*

*I just want to follow up on my interview with you today and let you know how much I appreciate your taking the time to meet with me. During our conversation, you mentioned several projects (name of company) is currently working on. It would be my pleasure to put some ideas together present to you. I look forward to hearing from you at your earliest convenience.*

*Sincerely,*

_____

## THANK YOU FOR LOOKING AT MY PROJECT/ SCRIPT/PROPOSAL

Dear Mr. _____:

Per our conversation, please find enclosed (project name, script title, proposal) for your consideration. I appreciate your taking the time to read it, and I look forward to hearing your thoughts.

If you have any questions, please don't hesitate to contact me.

Sincerely,

_____

Dear Ms. _____:

Thank you for returning my material with your notes and ideas. It isn't often that someone takes the time to go the extra mile, and I appreciate all your effort to help me. I'd love to keep the door open to send you my (projects/scripts/proposals) in the future.

A thousand thanks.

Best regards,

_____

## THANK YOU FOR SPEAKING ON MY BEHALF

Dear Mr. _____:

It meant the world to me that you took the time to speak on my behalf. Please know that not only do I appreciate your interrupting your busy day to help me, but I value the kind words you said about me.

Thank you.

Sincerely,

_____

## THANK YOU FOR LETTING US LOOK AT YOUR PROJECT/SCRIPT/PROPOSAL

Dear Ms. _____:

We really enjoyed reading *(name of your project/script/proposal)*, but unfortunately it isn't something we are in a position to pursue at this time. Please know we appreciate your thinking of us, and we wish you every success in your future endeavors.

Best regards,

_____

Dear Mr. _____:

Thank you so much for contacting us regarding your *(project/script/proposal)* for our consideration. Unfortunately, given the large number of submissions we receive on a daily basis, we are unable to accept unsolicited material. Please review our policies and procedures, which may be found on our website at *(insert web address)*. Thank you.

Best regards,

_____

## THANK YOU FOR THE INTERVIEW—MAYBE NEXT TIME

Dear Mr._____:

Thank you for updating me on the position at *(business name)*. Please know that if anything should change or if a new position becomes available, I would be interested in returning to meet with you. Thank you again for your time and consideration.

Sincerely,

_____

## THANK YOU FOR THE OFFER, BUT . . .

*Dear Mr._____:*

*It was an honor to receive your call offering me the position at (company name).*
*While I know working with you would be a wonderful experience for me,*
*I have chosen to pursue another opportunity at this time. Thank you very*
*much for considering me. I wish you the best of luck in finding the right*
*candidate for the position.*

*Sincerely,*

_____

## THANK YOU FOR YOUR CUSTOMER LOYALTY

*Dear Mrs. _____,*

*You have been a loyal customer of ours for the past (number of months/*
*years), and to show our appreciation we'd like to present you with the*
*enclosed (gift card/coupon) to be used on (Customer Appreciation Day/your*
*next purchase/at your convenience). Thank you for being a part of*
*(name of company) family.*

*Sincerely,*

*(name of president/owner)*

### GRATEFUL SAGE TIP

"Best regards" is the most common closing to use if you
are pursuing a career in the entertainment industry.

*Dear _____:*

*Thank you for the confidence you have placed in us. We are a company
dedicated to excellence in customer service, and your satisfaction is our top
priority. Please let us know if we can be of any further assistance to you. We
appreciate your trust.*

*Sincerely yours,*

---

*Dear Mr._____:*

*Thank you for your charitable donation to (name of charity). It is because of
generous gifts from good-hearted people like you that we are able to make a
significant difference in the lives of so many (children/people/seniors). Your
contribution will be used to (briefly mention use). From the bottom of our
hearts to yours, we thank you.*

*Sincerely,*

---

*Dear Ms. _____:*

*When your gift arrived at the office today, everyone cheered and
congregated in the conference room. I have never seen a group of dignified
people tear through (food item) in such a short amount of time. Thank you
for the delicious gift.*

*Sincerely,*

*Dear Mr._____:*

*What a pleasure it was to meet with you over lunch this afternoon. I think we accomplished a great deal, and I look forward to working together. If you have any further questions or concerns, please let me know. Thank you again for the excellent meal and conversation.*

*Sincerely,*

_____

*Dear _____:*

*As a small token of thanks for your hard work and continued loyalty at (name of business), please find enclosed a gift card to be used at the store, restaurant, or hotel of your choice. We recognize your dedication and we truly appreciate valuable associates like you. Thank you for contributing to our success.*

*Most sincerely,*

_____

## THE COLLEGIATE THANK-YOU

Your choice of school can have a profound effect on the rest of your life. Here, too, the thank-you note can make a difference, so be sure to send one within two days of your college interviews. Remember, thousands of people are applying for those few slots. It's possible that you could secure a spot based on the fact that you followed up and demonstrated responsibility, civility, and determination. Sending a thank-you note differentiates you and gives you a great opportunity to reiterate how much you want to receive an acceptance letter. It's also important to write thank-you notes to all the people who wrote letters of recommendation for you. If they took time to help you, they deserve to be thanked.

---

THANK YOU FOR THE LETTER OF RECOMMENDATION

---

*Dear Professor _____:*

*I am so extremely grateful to you for writing a letter of recommendation on my behalf. You are someone I hold in high regard and view with a tremendous amount of respect. Please know how much I appreciate your endorsement. I hope to use it not only for graduate school applications but in the business world as well. Thank you.*

*Most sincerely,*

---

*We make a living by what we get.*
*We make a life by what we give.*

—SIR WINSTON CHURCHILL, ENGLISH STATESMAN

# THE THANK-YOU THESAURUS
## POWER WORDS THAT MOVE MOUNTAINS

Use a thesaurus; you can find many ways to say the same thing, only better! Most word programs will have a built-in thesaurus.

ability ACCOMPLISHED aficionado
**authority** *brilliant* capable clout
COMMITTED competent connoisseur
CONSULTANT *creative* cultured
dedicated devoted educated enthusiastic
equipped experienced EXPERT
familiar fit **GIFTED** influence inspiration
KNOWLEDGEABLE POWER PRACTICED
professional proficient qualified **refined**
*skilled* skillful sophisticated specialist stylish
**TALENTED** technically savvy
veteran well-informed well-read
WELL-TRAVELED wiz

*" I've learned that people will forget what you said, people will forget what you did, but people will never forget how you made them feel. "*

—MAYA ANGELOU, AMERICAN POET AND NOVELIST

# CHAPTER 6

## SISTERHOODS AND SUPPORT CIRCLES

## THANK YOU FOR BEING A FRIEND

Sometimes the most precious gifts don't come in a box tied up with a beautiful bow, but are intangible gestures of love and support wrapped in the fabric of the heart. Whether you're going through a bad breakup, recovering from a loss, or embarking on a new adventure or an exciting phase of life, the gifts of kindness, friendship, and understanding are what make our lives richer and sweeter. So the next time you've gotten through with a little help from your friends, let them know how grateful you are for their understanding.

### GRATEFUL SAGE TIPS

When someone has done something nice for you, a great way to say thank you is to pay the kindness forward and pass the magic of gratitude on to someone else.

Try including a quote on friendship with your thank-you note. Those poets really do have a way with words!

**Ten Things Every Grateful Friend Should Know**

1. Do tell your friends how much you appreciate them.

2. Don't take your friends for granted.

3. Do acknowledge the little tokens of support you are given, and give them in return.

4. Don't ever be afraid to tell your friends how you feel. If they walk away, they were never true friends to begin with.

5. Do listen when people speak, and make eye contact. Even if you have nothing to say, they will feel you have heard them.

6. Don't ever be jealous of your friends' successes, love lives, or material possessions. We all have a different path to walk in life, so be inspired to achieve your own triumphs.

7. Do keep your friends' confidences. If your friends have entrusted you with private information, don't be a gossip. It's always wise to keep your personal details to yourself.

8. Don't be afraid to walk away from caustic people who belittle you or make you feel less than who you are.

9. Do encourage your friends to get help if they need it.

10. Do make time to celebrate life, love, and friendship. Eat and be merry with your friends—discover new worlds at museums and boutiques, and go to fabulous destinations!

## WRITING THANK-YOUS OF FRIENDSHIP

It's true that handwritten notes are always best, but when it comes to friendship, saying thank you can take many forms beyond the formalities of pen and paper and social protocol. Often it is the unexpected thank-you that warms our hearts and touches our souls.

❋ Handwritten cards and notes sent through the mail often surprise the recipient with a burst of appreciation because they really are thoughtful and intimate.

❋ Small gifts make excellent thank-yous and need not be expensive. If your friend loves to garden, a small package of flower seeds or an orchid plant really shows your thoughtfulness. The possibilities are endless!

❋ Edible thank-yous are delicious, too, whether home baked or from the corner bakery or candy shop.

❋ Emailed thank-yous are always kind, especially ones created with one of the dozens of online greeting card sites and apps that include music and animation. Tip: Do an Internet search or take a look at www.Hallmark.com, www.AmericanGreetings.com, or www.BlueMountain.com. You'll find some amazing heartfelt and hilarious options to choose from.

❋ Who doesn't adore gorgeous flowers, fragrant candles, fabulous chocolate, or festive Champagne? These are always sweet thank-you options!

*Great minds discuss ideas;*
*average minds discuss events;*
*small minds discuss people.*

—ELEANOR ROOSEVELT,
AMERICAN AUTHOR AND FIRST LADY

GRATEFUL SAGE TIP

L'chaim—In Hebrew it means *to life!* Celebrate the laugh lines and embrace your wrinkles! They are outward signs of the smiles you have given to others and the joy you have expressed along your life's journey. Be grateful for every single breath you take, treasure each day the sun rises, and share your magic.

## QUIPS FROM GRATEFUL SAGES
## THROUGH THE AGES

*Have no friends not equal to yourself.*
—CONFUCIUS, CHINESE PHILOSOPHER

*Friendship with oneself is all important, because without it one
cannot be friends with anyone else in the world.*
—ELEANOR ROOSEVELT, AMERICAN AUTHOR AND FIRST LADY

*It is not so much our friends' help that helps us as the confident
knowledge that they will help us.*
—EPICURUS, GREEK PHILOSOPHER

*God gave us our relatives; thank God we can choose our friends.*
—ETHEL WATTS MUMFORD, AMERICAN NOVELIST
AND PLAYWRIGHT

*I count myself in nothing else so happy as in a soul remembering my
good friends.*
—WILLIAM SHAKESPEARE, ELIZABETHAN POET AND
PLAYWRIGHT, *KING RICHARD II*

*The only reward of virtue is virtue; the only way to have a friend is
to be one.*
—RALPH WALDO EMERSON, TRANSCENDENTALIST WRITER

*True friendship is a plant of slow growth, and must undergo
and withstand the shocks of adversity before it is entitled
to the appellation.*
—GEORGE WASHINGTON, FIRST UNITED STATES PRESIDENT

## THANK YOU FOR BEING A FRIEND—
## SAMPLE NOTES

Here you will find notes to help you reach out and touch someone who has reached out to you. Use these words of appreciation for the people who have helped you through the rough patches in life.

---

### THANKS FOR BEING THERE

*Dear _____,*

*How can I ever thank you for always being there for me? You are a true friend, and I am forever grateful. Thank you.*

*With appreciation,*

*_____*

---

### THANKS FOR BEING MY GREEK SISTER

*Dear _____,*

*It has been both an honor and a privilege to be your (name of sorority) sister. Through all the exchanges, excitement, studying, and fraternity activity, you are someone I know will always be there for me. Thank you for being in my life.*

*(Sorority name) love,*

*_____*

## THANKS FOR BEING MY SOUL SISTER

Dear _____,

*We've laughed until we've cried and we've held each other tightly. I feel so blessed that we've walked this life together and shared in each other's joys and sorrows. From the bottom of my heart, thank you for being my sister and my best friend.*

*Love,*

_____

## THANKS FOR OUR ROCK-SOLID FRIENDSHIP

Dear _____,

*You are the best! No matter what's happening, you are always someone I can count on through thick and thin. I don't think you'll ever know how much I appreciate your gracious heart and the courageous spirit that always makes me smile. You have affected my life on so many levels. I am truly a better person because of you. Thank you!*

*Yours truly,*

_____

## THANKS FOR SAVING ME FROM MYSELF

Dear _____,

*Thank you for holding me up when I didn't think I was going to make it. Thank you for showing me there really is a light at the end of the tunnel. Thank you for reminding me to count my blessings. Thank you for explaining that time heals all wounds. Thank you for just letting me cry and not judging me for it.. Thank you, my friend.*

*Love,*

_____

THANKS, JUST BECAUSE

*Dear _____,*
*I want you to know that you mean the world to me. Thank you for being*
*my best friend.*
*With my love,*

_____

*Dear _____,*
*There are simply no words to express the depth of my gratitude . . .*
*Thank you,*

_____

## THE GOLDEN RULES OF TEXTING

Nothing replaces a great conversation with a good friend in person or on the phone, but sometimes when you're in a hurry, only texting will do!

* ❋ Remember that texting is more personal than email because it is instantaneous and shows up right away on the recipient's mobile device. If what you have to say can wait, send an email.

* ❋ Remember that you can turn off the "read receipt" in your message settings if you don't want the person who sent you a text to know when you read it.

* ❋ Remember that when you text, the person you are texting can't see your face or hear your voice, so the spirit of what you are trying to say might be misinterpreted. For example, if you text something you think is funny to a friend, the other person might not realize you are just joking around and could be upset! When in doubt, decide against sending a text that might be taken the wrong way.

❀ Remember never to text or gossip about anyone. Why? Because gossiping is just plain wrong. If you need a practical reason, if that person sees the text you sent, you might end up in trouble over it.

❀ Remember to avoid group emails! Sometimes you may not be aware of everyone who is on the group text, and you might send an embarrassing message back in error!

❀ Remember never to text and drive a car, text and ride a bicycle, or text and walk. It's really easy to get caught up in the texting, quickly stop paying attention to where you are, and hurt yourself or someone else. Every single text can wait!

❀ If you write something in **CAPS**, (or in **bold type**), it can be perceived that you are sending a **SCREAMING TEXT.**

## THE ACRONYM DICTIONARY: DIGITAL TEXTING

| 2MORO | Tomorrow |
|-------|----------|
| 2NITE | Tonight |
| B4N | Bye for Now |
| BFF | Best Friends Forever |
| BRB | Be Right Back |
| BTW | By the Way |
| CYA | See Ya |
| GR8 | Great |
| HW | Homework |
| IDK | I Don't Know |
| ILY | I Love You |
| IMO | In My Opinion |
| JK | Just Kidding |
| K | Okay |
| LOL | Laughing Out Loud |
| LTR | Later |

| MV | Movie |
|---|---|
| NP | No Problem |
| O | Hug |
| OIC | Oh, I See |
| OMG | Oh, My Gosh! |
| OMW | On My Way |
| R | Are |
| RBTL | Read Between the Lines |
| ROFL | Rolling on the Floor Laughing |
| RT | Retweet |
| THX or THKS | Thanks |
| TMI | Too Much Information |
| TTYL | Talk to You Later |
| TY | Thank You! |
| TYVM | Thank You Very Much |
| U | You |
| WDYT | What Do You Think? |
| WE | Whatever |
| WYWH | Wish You Were Here |
| X | Kiss |
| XOXO | Hugs And Kisses |
| YOLO | You Only Live Once |

*I met in the street a very poor young man who was in love. His hat was old, his coat worn, his cloak was out at the elbows, the water passed through his shoes—and the stars through his soul.*

—VICTOR HUGO, FRENCH WRITER AND POET

# CHAPTER 7

## LOVE AND ROMANCE

## THANK YOU FROM THE BOTTOM OF MY HEART

One of our greatest human needs is to be loved by another and feel appreciated. Romantic scribes have known for centuries that the key to capturing a loved one's heart begins with a passionate letter declaring their love and admiration. With stars in their eyes, they bare their souls, risking rejection to give the gift of gratitude to another hopeful heart. After all, in essence a love letter is really a proclamation thanking someone for how they make you feel. In today's world, lovers sometimes forget that acknowledging the importance of the other person in their lives is key. Those two small words—"thank you"—are so powerful, they can make, break, or reinforce a relationship. It is essential that we make a habit of using them daily. So the next time you've got a prince on the line, send him a "Thank You from the Bottom of My Heart" note. It's guaranteed to help seal the deal!

### WRITING THE ROMANTIC THANK-YOU

When it comes to writing tender notes of love and appreciation, there aren't any set rules. The most important thing to do is simply write down your feelings of gratitude and send them. What matters are the passionate words that come from your heart. Sometimes it feels difficult to express what we feel, or we feel ridiculous writing something that seems overly dramatic or too emotional. But just a few words can have a tremendous impact. You don't have to write pages—even a loving phrase will do.

**Ideas to Help Keep Love's Light in Your Life!**

* Send a handwritten thank-you love note on your favorite stationery with a quick spray of your perfume, and he'll surely think of you. Maybe a sweet lipstick kiss on the envelope will make his heart feel yours, too.

* There are hundreds of stationery choices, from creative and funny store-bought cards to elegant, finely crafted, and handmade paper.

* Send a postcard with a short little note, love quote, or poem. He'll get the message!

* Emails and e-cards are always appreciated and add sparkle to your loved one's day. Check out some of the online greeting card websites.

* Text messaging is wonderful instant communication for letting that special someone know you're thinking of him, too. C U LTR

* Slip a note into your sweetheart's briefcase, pocket, suitcase, or car. He'll be surprised when he finds it and grateful to know you took the time to do something special.

* Don't forget that your appreciation can extend beyond a written thank-you note. Hugs, kisses, holding hands, and eye contact are all ways to connect with that gratitude attitude. Actions really can speak louder than words.

* My mother always said, "The way to a man's heart is through his stomach." It really is true. Cook a fabulous candlelight dinner, send a basket of homemade chocolate chip cookies, or make a picnic for the seaside to show him you appreciate him.

✽ According to marriage and family therapists Drs. Lew and Gloria Richfield, authors of *Together Forever: 125 Loving Ways to Have a Vital and Romantic Marriage*, "Mail a love letter to your partner. With a stamp. Love letters shouldn't stop just because you live at the same address."

## TIMING IS EVERYTHING

Yes, it is a good thing to demonstrate your feelings, otherwise you'd never know if he feels the same way about you, too. At the same time, you want to be a lady and let the gentleman court you. In the beginning of a relationship, some men might feel a woman is coming on too strongly if she sends a barrage of fan mail, so use your best judgment. You'll know when the time is right.

If you have no intention of seeing a guy again following your first date, then let the verbal "thank you" given at the end of the evening suffice. Don't send an email or text the next day thanking him again, because he might think you're interested in him. If he follows up and you aren't interested, simply let him know you appreciated the date and don't set up a future one.

On the other hand, if you think you've met your match, wait and see what happens. After a few dates, you'll probably have each other's emails, and it would be appropriate to send a note saying something thoughtful like,

*Aric,*
*When I said I always wished to have Champagne over New York City, I never dreamed it would come true. Sipping bubbles high atop a garden rooftop was an experience I'll never forget. Thank you for caring enough to make my dream come true. Here's to many more star-filled nights.*
*With affection,*
*Kelly*

Acknowledging the effort your potential love interest makes causes that magical gift of gratitude to continue. People want to keep giving when they feel appreciated for their efforts, because it makes them feel good inside. So whatever you decide to do, be creative and do it well, so those love blessings keep coming to you!

## Ten Relationship Keys Every Woman Should Know

1. Do remember that if you don't *love and respect yourself first*, no one else will.

2. Don't try to change someone into what you think the person should be, and don't let anyone try to change you into someone you aren't.

3. Do be appreciative and acknowledge even the small efforts your love interest makes.

4. Don't stay in a relationship if you are unhappy or not being treated the way you deserve. Life is simply too short. Whom you choose to spend your life and time with is your decision.

5. Do help and support each other without being demanding.

6. Don't be afraid to forgive. It releases your anger and allows you to love again.

7. Do remember that to make a relationship strong, both of you must participate, listen, and communicate equally.

8. Don't try to rescue someone whose problems require professional help.

9. Do observe how your potential mate treats others (especially his mother); he will treat you the same way.

10. Do give love generously without expectations.

## QUIPS FROM GRATEFUL AND AFFECTIONATE SAGES THROUGH THE AGES

*In writing or speaking, give to every person his due title. The deepest principle in human nature is the craving to be appreciated.*

—WILLIAM JAMES,
AMERICAN PSYCHOLOGIST AND PHILOSOPHER

*Thou art to me a delicious torment.*

—RALPH WALDO EMERSON, TRANSCENDENTALIST WRITER

*Associate yourself with men of good quality if you esteem your own reputation; for 'tis better to be alone than in bad company.*

—GEORGE WASHINGTON, FIRST UNITED STATES PRESIDENT

*Men are like wine: some turn to vinegar, but the best improve with age.*

—POPE JOHN XXIII

*There is no remedy for love but to love more.*

—HENRY DAVID THOREAU, AMERICAN AUTHOR

*Ignorant men don't know what good they hold in their hands until they've flung it away.*

—SOPHOCLES, CLASSICAL GREEK PLAYWRIGHT

*Let us be grateful to people who make us happy. They are the charming gardeners who make our souls blossom.*

—MARCEL PROUST, FRENCH NOVELIST

# THE INTERNATIONAL LANGUAGE OF LOVE THESAURUS

| | |
|---|---|
| Afrikaans | Ek het jou lief |
| Armenian | Yes kez sirum em |
| English | I love you |
| Chinese | Wǒ ài nǐ |
| Cree | Kisakihitin |
| Creole | Mi aime jou |
| French | Je t'aime |
| German | Ich liebe dich |
| Greek | S'agapo |
| Hawaiian | Aloha wau ia`oe |
| Irish (Gaelic) | Ta gra agam ort |
| Italian | Ti amo |
| Japanese | Ai'shiteru yo |
| Polish | Kocham cie |
| Russian | Ya tebya liubliu |
| Spanish | Te amo |
| Swahili | Nakupenda |
| Swedish | Jag älskar dig |
| Welsh | Rwy'n dy garu di |
| Yiddish | Ikh hob dikh lib |

# SHAKESPEAREAN PHRASES OF LOVE AND DEVOTION

*In thy face I see the map of honor, truth, and loyalty.*

—*HENRY VI, PART TWO*

*My heart is ever at your service, my lord.*

—*TIMON OF ATHENS*

*Love looks not with the eyes, but with the mind; And therefore is wing'd Cupid painted blind.*

—*A MIDSUMMER NIGHT'S DREAM*

*Now join your hands, and with your hands your hearts.*

—*KING HENRY VI*

*They do not love that do not show their love.*

—*TWO GENTLEMEN OF VERONA*

*The course of true love never did run smooth.*

—*A MIDSUMMER NIGHT'S DREAM*

## STRAIGHTEN YOUR CROWN: SOCIAL MEDIA AND TEXTING TIPS

Social media is a fabulous avenue to interact in the global arena, promote a cause, post pictures of your adventures, or celebrate your success. Here are some tips to remember when you are out in the world looking for your soul mate!

✿ Do be mysterious! You know that the minute you meet someone who sparks your fancy, you search their online profile right away to get their background details. Chances are, they are doing the exact same search on you. So if you want to keep your personal details to yourself, set your social media profiles to private and delete the unnecessary details. Then run an Internet search on yourself, so you can see how much of your personal digital content is public and adjust it accordingly, if necessary.

❁ Do stay off your mobile device while you are on a date and keep it in your pocket or handbag. If you have to check your phone, excuse yourself after dinner and check it in the ladies room. If someone has asked to spend time with you, give them the courtesy of your attention.

❁ Don't be a stalker and spy on someone else's social media account and don't make up a fake account so they won't know you are keeping tabs on their online activities.

❁ Do remember that if you are friends with your ex-boyfriend or ex-girlfriend on social media, your new love interest may wonder if you still have feelings for that person or if your ex might still have feelings for you. Just keep it in mind when a former love "likes" your post, starts "following" you, or makes comments on your page. Sometimes it's better to leave the past behind.

❁ Don't send a breakup text message unless you simply can't end the relationship in person.

❁ Do remember, texting tends to be more intimate than email as it allows a direct notification to someone's mobile device and (unless you change the settings) shows the sender that their text has been delivered and read. If you want to keep that boundary of not allowing someone to know the exact moment you have read their message, make sure you turn off the "read receipt" that appears to the sender.

❁ Don't post cryptic breakup messages online about your love life or negative comments about a former flame for the world to see. If it wasn't meant to be, straighten your crown,

smile, and move on. The best revenge is happiness—
besides, you are one step closer to finding your true love.

❊ Do remember to give thoughtful consideration when
posting or updating your relationship status. Suddenly,
you've made your relationship official, and your post might
be premature.

## THANK YOU FROM THE BOTTOM OF MY HEART—SAMPLE NOTES

When it comes to love and romance, there's nothing like a well-timed thank-you note to rekindle an old flame, ignite a new one, or let Mr. Right's parents know you're the one.

### THANK YOU FOR LOVING ME

*Darling _____,*
*To thoughtful you, from thankful me! Thank you for leaving your*
*(smile/handprint) on my heart.*

_____

*XOXO*

*Dear _____,*
*You make me feel like I'm the only woman in this whole wide world.*
*Thank you for loving me.*
*Love,*

_____

*Dear _____,*
*How can I convey my appreciation for the love and magic*
*you send my way?*

_____

*Dear _____,*
*There are simply no words to express how grateful*
*I am to have you in my life . . .*
*With all my love and affection,*

———————

*Dear _____,*
*You are my everything.*
*XOXO*

———————

*Dear _____,*
*In your hands you hold my heart.*
*I love you.*

———————

THANK YOU FOR BEING MY FRIEND

*Dear _____,*
*Thank you for loving me for who I am and never, ever trying to change me.*
*Thank you for allowing me the freedom to pursue my dreams and believing*
*that I really can do anything. Thank you for applauding my victories and*
*catching me when I fall. Thank you for being my best friend. I adore you.*
*Love,*

———————

## THANK YOU FOR THE FLOWERS

Dear _____,

What a wonderful surprise! When those beautiful flowers came down the hall, I really thought they were for someone else. They were so stunning, I couldn't believe it when they stopped at my desk—then I saw my name on the card. My heart pounded and swelled with emotion when I read your sweet words. Thank you for making me the most envied woman in the office!

I love you, too . . .

XOXO

_____

## THANK YOU, JUST BECAUSE

Dear _____,

When I was a little girl, I dreamed about what you'd be like. I looked into the heavens every night and wondered where you were and how and when we'd meet. I begged the stars to keep you safe and for the moon to light your way to me. As I stand next to you now and gaze into your eyes, I am so incredibly thankful I met you that starry, starry night.

With all my love,

_____

## THANK YOU TO MR. RIGHT'S PARENTS

This kind of thank-you note would lend itself to an air of higher formality than a casual love note.

> *Dear Mr. and Mrs. _____,*
>
> *It's been such a pleasure getting to know both of you over the past year. I really appreciate your welcoming me into your home and always including me in your family plans. I especially enjoyed helping in the kitchen and cooking that delicious (name of holiday) dinner. Thank you for making me feel so special.*
>
> *Sincerely yours,*
>
> _____

## THANK YOU FOR THE GIFT

> *Dear _____,*
>
> *I am forever grateful to you for your thoughtful and generous gift. I know it comes from your gracious heart to mine.*
>
> *A thousand kisses . . .*
>
> *Love,*
>
> _____

## THANK YOU FOR DINNER

Dear _____,

How do you always think of the most wonderful things to do? I loved having dinner with you last night at (name of place/beach/park). It was such a fun idea and I really, really enjoyed being with you. Thank you for making it an amazing evening.

With affection,

_____

## THANK YOU FOR LOVING ME, GOOD-BYE

Dear _____,

This note is hard for me to write because I love you. I have felt so honored to have you in my life, and I am eternally grateful to have had the chance to know you. I wish our timing were different, because if we had met in another place and time, who knows what could have been? Thank you for loving me so much that you are willing to let me go. I will remember you always.

Love,

_____

" *You don't love someone for their looks, or their clothes, or their fancy car, but because they sing a song only you can hear.* "

—OSCAR WILDE, IRISH WRITER AND POET

# CHAPTER 8

## WEDDING BELLS AND THANK-YOUS

## I DO, I DO, AND THANK YOU, TOO

From the moment we brides say yes, we are swept up into a white wave of wedding traditions, rituals, parties, and presents, all of which require thank-you notes. At this time, probably more than at any other, we have a great deal to be thankful for. That means writing a huge number of thank-you notes! Don't be selfish and write them all yourself; let your groom share in writing them, too. From the engagement party to the bachelorette party, the bridal shower, the wedding, the honeymoon, and beyond into the first year of marriage, we are expressing our gratitude and appreciation for the support, love, and generosity that we enjoy from our friends and family at this special time.

### THE GRATEFUL BRIDE'S GUIDE TO THANK-YOU SUCCESS

The last thing you want to think about on your honeymoon is the mountain of thank-you notes that have to be sent out upon your return home. It can be utterly overwhelming. By taking just a few simple steps before the big day, you can really reduce the worry and feel free to dance the night away without a single twinge of bridal-gratitude guilt. At your shower, you probably had someone writing down everything you received and the name of the person who gave it to you. After the wedding, it is often difficult to be so organized. There is no way in the world you will be able to remember who gave you what gift and when. Here are a few ideas to help you savor every moment.

* Many brides keep a file that contains a card for each invited guest with all their pertinent contact information. Other brides keep a list of gifts received and thank-you notes sent. If you can't find the time to do either of these, simply take the gift card and mark the date you received the gift, what the gift was, and the address of the sender. You can also cut the return address from the box or envelope and tape it to the gift card. After you write the thank-you note, mark the card with a check and include the date, in case you need to go back and verify that you sent the note.

* If the gift was shipped directly from a store, there should be a shipping receipt inside or affixed to a clear plastic window on the outside of the package. If there isn't a separate gift message inside the package, refer to the shipping receipt for the sender information and the details about exchanges or returns. Make sure to make a note on the receipt once you have sent your thank-you note for the gift. Use one of your gift boxes for the gift cards that need thank-you notes and another one for the ones you've sent.

* Try to do a few thank-you notes every day so you don't get overwhelmed. (Don't forget, people can send you gifts for up to a year.) Better yet, get your new spouse to write a few with you. Open a bottle of bubbly, order in, and make it fun!

* Order or purchase your stationery in advance so you're ready to go when you return from your honeymoon. Get a package of black or blue ink pens at the same time so you are prepared.

✱ If you're thinking about managing your guest list online or on a spreadsheet, also consider creating a "group" in your address book contacts for your wedding guest list and customizing fields for RSVPs, meal preference, gift received, and thank-you note sent! Then your information will be synced to your mobile device and will allow you to send a gift acknowledgment through a stationery app with a gorgeous picture from your honeymoon!

✱ Your gift registry should designate one address for gifts to be sent to, to help avoid lost gifts and misplaced cards at your reception.

## THE GRATEFUL BRIDE'S THANK-YOU CHECKLIST

Traditionally, the bridal thank-you note is formal, handwritten in black or blue ink, and should be sent within three months of the wedding.

1. The appropriate formal stationery to use is of good quality and ecru or white in color with a matching envelope. Pastel colors have also become acceptable. Consider ordering your thank-you notes when you order your wedding invitations.

2. The traditional bride's fold-over or "informal" note is approximately 5¼″ x 3½″ and is typically personalized with your name or monogram.

3. Compose a draft on the computer of what you want to say before handwriting the actual note. Because brides have so many notes to write, you can use the same note and personalize it for each individual.

4. You'll be writing a lot of notes, so there is a tendency to become repetitive, which can make your thank-you sound stale and generic. Refer to "The Thank-You Thesaurus" to give yourself some fresh ideas. There are many ways to say the same thing, only better!

5. Use lined paper underneath your note so your writing follows a straight line. You can also use a ruler or anything with a straight edge to guide your pen. And leave yourself room on the page—don't jam it all together!

6. Before you seal the envelope, read your note out loud to make sure you didn't miss a word or two. Always double check the spelling of the name and address.

7. If you have a large wedding with hundreds of guests, consider sending out "gift acknowledgment" cards, so people will know that their gifts have been received and that a thank-you note is on the way. This gives you more time to write a proper thank-you note.

8. Don't send email thank-you notes for wedding gifts or post a blanket thank-you on your wedding website. If someone took the time to send you a gift, their efforts should be thanked accordingly.

9. Do remember that a separate thank-you note should be sent for gifts you received at your bridal shower.

10. Don't use your bad handwriting as an excuse not to send a thank-you! If you absolutely must, you can go the computer-generated route, use a script font like Monotype Corsiva, print your thank-you notes on gorgeous stationery, and then personally sign them.

11. Brides should sign with their maiden name before the wedding and married name (if they are using it) after the wedding.

## AVOIDING LATE THANK-YOU NOTE ANXIETY

If you happen to miss sending a thank-you note within that three-month period or close to it, try to be gracious about the error. Write something like, "In all the excitement of the wedding, I somehow managed to separate your gift from your card . . ." or "Many apologies for the tardiness of my note. As you can imagine, we are still getting used to married life . . ."

❀ Don't delay your thank-you notes with the excuse that you're waiting to include your wedding picture. Just send them! Check out the online stationery apps like www.RedStamp.com that will upload your favorite images, access your contacts, allow you to write your thank-you notes, and print and mail them for you with a stamp!

❀ Call people who ship you gifts, so they aren't left wondering if their presents arrived. It really deflates gift givers if you don't acknowledge the spirit of excitement they are expecting you to have when you receive their presents. If you absolutely can't call, do send an email to acknowledge you received the shipment—then follow up with a thank-you note.

## MONOGRAMS

Monograms are always in style and represent a certain sense of tradition and class. Don't be afraid to use them; they add elegance to the presentation of your thank-you notes.

Before the wedding, you would use your first, middle, and maiden name.

*Margaret Mary Poisson*

If you are using initials that are all the same height, they should follow the order of your name. Your monogram would look like this:

*MMP*

If you are using initials that vary in height, your last name would be in the middle:

*MPM.*

After the wedding, your new last name is incorporated into your monogram. Your maiden name will move into the position of your middle name, and your married name will take the place of your maiden name.

*Margaret Poisson Learman*

If you are using initials of the same size, your new monogram would look like this:

*MPL*

With initials of different heights, your new initial (for your married name) will be in the middle:

*MLP*

## THE ELECTRONIC THANK-YOU

If you are thinking about sending out email thank-you notes for your wedding gifts, remember that only the classic, handwritten thank-you note is the most acceptable for this momentous occasion. Blanket email thank-yous or enthusiastic posts on your wedding website do not substitute for thanking each and every person individually for their generous gifts to you.

## RETURNING GIFTS

Even though you registered, it's inevitable that someone will give you something that simply isn't your style and must be returned. Here are some ideas for how to handle this delicately:

1. Avoid telling the gift-giver unless the item is broken or damaged. Do your best to return the gift to the store of purchase; hold on to the packaging if there is no gift receipt.

2. Really consider the gift giver's feelings before you return a gift. If the gift is from your new mother-in-law, you might want to consider holding on to it to foster good relations.

3. If you can't return or exchange a gift and you really can't bear to keep it, consider donating it or giving it to someone who would cherish it.

4. As a last resort, try reselling the item; eBay is a wonderful selling tool.

## WEDDING WEBSITES

Take advantage of the electronic revolution and create your own digital domain to streamline your wedding bell bliss. Wedding websites are all the rage and allow you to upload your personal content, pictures, and event details, and manage guest RSVPs, gift registries, #hashtags, and social media links with up-to-the-minute, behind-the-scenes news. Take a look at all your options online.

## SOCIAL MEDIA WEDDING AND #HASHTAGGING TIPS

Weddings are exciting moments in our lives, and in the joy of seeing you say "I do!," your guests will snap away with their cameras and mobile devices, clamoring to be the first to record and upload your diamond memories on social media sites for all to see. In the spirit of sharing your joy with others who aren't there to participate in celebrating your blessings in person, your family and friends show the best and most loving intentions. Even so, let's face it, things can get out of hand. So here are some tips to help keep your wedding magnificently ceremonial:

* Define your social media rules before your wedding. Pictures are a welcome gift, but politely ask your guests to wait until the ceremony has concluded before they post online, so they can be present in the sacredness of the ritual they were asked to witness. Additionally, extra flashing lights might interfere with your professional photographer's pictures.

* Designate a specific wedding profile social media page to direct your guests to, to gather your posts into a central media location. If an unflattering picture is posted on your page, it gives you more control to delete it if necessary.

* Promote your wedding #hashtag so when your guests post images on social media sites at your wedding, they have a designated #hashtag ready to use and a searchable link to call up the pictures. When you create your tag, make sure it is unique to you and do a hashtag search to make sure no one else has used it. #MrandMrsBrowne2016

* Offering event venue WiFi to your guests and printing the access information on table cards, or writing it creatively on a chalkboard with your #hashtag, will help you get table pictures of friends and family your photographer might miss. These moments celebrating joyous occasions in life become treasured memories, so encourage your guests to please enjoy the moment and spend the time with you—and not their phones and other devices!

✻ Create your "check-in" at your wedding venue before the big day, so when your guests start posting they can link their heartfelt congratulations and effortlessly post your nuptial pics.

✻ Do check out the amazing array of wedding ideas that can be found on dozens of nuptial-themed sites and idea boards online, like www.Pinterest.com.

✻ Remember, you can use technology in your favor! For your loved ones who can't attend your sacred vows, you can live stream the ceremony via video chat sites like Skype or FaceTime and reach locations all around the world. It's also a brilliant way to remotely open your gifts together and stay connected to the people you love and cherish.

✻ Crane's *The Wedding Blue Book* and *The Blue Book of Stationery* are excellent resources for all brides! Visit www. Crane.com.

## WEDDING FAVORS—
## FAVORITE CHARITY DONATION

Your wedding day will be filled with wonderful moments and magical memories. To thank the most important people in your life or honor loved ones who join you from the heavens, make a donation for your wedding favors and simply print this information on a card. This is a heartfelt way to begin a new life together while making a difference. Make up your own verse or scout the amazing ideas and phrasing shared by hundreds of grateful couples online.

*In lieu of favors, a donation to (name of charity)
has been made in your honor and to celebrate our
loved ones who join us in spirit. From the bottom of
our hearts, thank you for the blessings you have
given us and for being a treasured part of our lives.
(Name of Bride and Groom)
(Wedding Date)*

# THE GLOBAL THANK-YOU THESAURUS

—◁○▷—

| | |
|---|---|
| Afrikaans | Dankie |
| Armenian | Shenorhakal yem |
| Chinese (Mandarin) | Toa chie |
| Dutch | Dank je |
| English | Thank you |
| French | Merci beaucoup |
| German | Danke schoen |
| Greek | Efharistó |
| Hebrew | Toda |
| Hungarian | Kösz, Köszönöm |
| Irish (Gaelic) | Go raibh maith agat |
| Italian | Grazie |
| Japanese | Arigato |
| Norwegian | Takk |
| Polish | Dziekuje |
| Portuguese | Obrigado |
| Spanish | Muchas gracias |
| Swahili | Asante |
| Swedish | Tack |
| Welsh | Diolc |

# I DO, I DO, AND THANK YOU, TOO— SAMPLE NOTES

Here are some thank-you notes to help you let everybody in your extended wedding party know how much their contribution to your new life means to both of you.

## THANK YOU TO THE BRIDE'S PARENTS FOR THE WEDDING

*Dear Mom and Dad,*

*Words cannot describe my sincere appreciation to you both for giving (name of spouse) and me the wedding of our dreams. Thank you for every single detail you made possible, for your patience when mine wore thin, the advice you never thought I heard, the unconditional love you adored me with, and—quite simply—for just being there. I will always be your little girl. With all my love,*

_____

## CANDLESTICKS

*Dear _____,*

*(Name of spouse) joins me in thanking you for the gorgeous candlesticks! We just love them. We will think of you over every romantic candlelight dinner . . . well, not every one! Thank you so very much. With love,*

_____

Dear _____,

*We are overwhelmed by your generous gift. You couldn't possibly imagine how many (china or dinnerware) patterns we looked at before we finally picked this one. We will think of you both every time we use our fabulous dishes! Thank you!*

*Sincerely,*

_____

Dear Mr. and Mrs. _____,

*We just can't thank you enough for the spectacular cookware! You know we love to cook, and with all the cookbooks we received, we're sure to be in fierce competition with world-class chefs. Now we can make all the very best gourmet meals. After we've had a chance to practice a recipe or two, we'd love to have you both over for dinner. (Name of spouse) joins me in thanking you.*

*Sincerely yours,*

_____

Dear _____,

*I believe the kitchen is the heartbeat of the home--where celebrations are created and cherished recipes shared. Thank you for the gorgeous cookware that will hold my love as I create the gift of giving these treasured moments to my new family.*

*With all my love,*

_____

CRYSTAL GLASSWARE

Dear Mr. and Mrs._____,

When I met (name of spouse), I felt as though I had stumbled upon the most sparkling thing in the world. That is, until we opened your gift last night. Thank you for the crystal glasses—they are just magnificent. We were so excited that we opened a very special bottle of Champagne and toasted you for your love and thoughtfulness! Cheers!

Love,

_____

FILL IN THE BLANKS

Dear Mr. and Mrs._____,

The one thing we desperately needed was (name of gift). You would not believe how many times we have already used it this week alone. Thank you so much—we just love it! More important, thank you from the bottom of our hearts for sharing this special day with us.

Sincerely,

_____

Dear Mr. and Mrs. _____,

I know I thanked you at the reception, but I want to let you both know how much we appreciate the lovely (name of gift) you gave us. We hope you had a wonderful time at our wedding . . . it meant so much to us that you were there to help celebrate our new life together. Thank you!

With affection,

_____

## FRAME

*Dear Mr. and Mrs. _____,*

*Thank you so much for the beautiful frame! We really wanted a special one for our wedding picture, and this one is just stunning. Please know that when we look at it, we will think of your generosity. We hope you had a wonderful time at the wedding and thank you for joining us.*

*Most sincerely,*

_____

## FOOD PROCESSOR, STAND MIXER, OR BLENDER

*Dear _____,*

*We never dreamed in a million years we would ever get the (food processor, stand mixer, or blender)! You have single-handedly cut our kitchen time in half and helped us create delicious (meals/smoothies). We can't wait to have you over to celebrate love, great food, and wonderful friends! Hope you had as terrific a time at the wedding as we did! Our most sincere thanks!*

*Love,*

_____

## GIFT CERTIFICATES AND GIFT CARDS

*Dear _____,*

*You can't imagine our excitement when we opened your gift! Thank you so much for your very generous gift card. Now we can go on a shopping spree and get everything we need to set up our home together. We are just thrilled! From the bottom of our hearts, thank you.*

*Gratefully yours,*

_____

## HONEYMOON GIFT CARD—
## HOTEL, AIRLINE, OR TRAVEL

Dear _____,

Oh, thank you so very much! Your presence at our wedding was a gift in itself, but the gift card to the (name of hotel, airline, travel company) for our honeymoon is simply spectacular. We so appreciate your generosity toward the honeymoon of our dreams and every single blessing you sent our way. Thank you for giving us the gift of a memory together that we will cherish for a lifetime. With our love and thanks,

_____

## MONOGRAMMED TOWELS

Dear _____,

What a perfect and lovely gift! Thank you for the gorgeous cotton towels. We desperately needed matching ones and having a set complete with our new monogram feels simply luxurious. We hope you had a wonderful time at our wedding—it meant so much to us to have you there. With love,

_____

## PLATTER OR SERVING DISH

Dear _____,

What a gorgeous (platter/serving dish)! No matter what we serve on it, it's going to look delicious, and that's half the battle! We love it and look forward to using it at our next festive occasion. Thank you so much for thinking of us and for being such good friends. Sincerely,

_____

## SILVER, SILVER PLATE, OR SILVER PLACE SETTING

Dear _____,

*(Name of spouse) and I screamed when we opened your "sterling" gift. We absolutely love the silver (name of item)! We just can't express how grateful we are; (it is/they are) simply lovely. We will definitely enjoy (it/them) on each and every special occasion.*

*Thank you!*

_____

## VASE

Dear Mr. and Mrs. _____,

*You can't imagine how excited we were when we opened your gift. The one thing we really wanted was a beautiful vase! It is so stunning that we immediately placed it on the mantel over the fireplace. Now we have a really great excuse to keep the living room filled with beautiful flowers. Thank you so much for thinking of us and helping us celebrate our wedding.*

*With love,*

_____

## REVEREND, PRIEST, RABBI

*Dear (Reverend, Father, or Rabbi),*

*It is with great joy that I write this note to thank you for performing the wedding ceremony for (name of spouse) and me. We so appreciated the time you took to meet with us and make sure that every element of the ceremony was just right. I know that marriage can be trying at times, but we truly feel that with the tools of honor, communication, and trust you have shared with us, we are sure to be prepared for anything that comes our way. Thank you so very much for cementing our bond to each other.*

*Respectfully yours,*

_____

## TO THE GROOM'S PARENTS FOR THE REHEARSAL DINNER

*Dear Mom and Dad,*

*I want you to know how much I appreciated the rehearsal dinner you gave us—it was magnificent in every way. A special night, surrounded by only our closest of family and friends, it filled our hearts with joy and made us feel like the luckiest couple in the whole world. As you rose to toast us, I swelled with emotion, reflecting on every single moment you've given me to create my wonderful life. As I look forward to creating a new chapter, please know it is built on the foundation of the virtues of love and gratitude you have instilled in me.*

*With my love, always,*

_____

## Happily Ever After Anniversary Gifts

| YEAR | TRADITIONAL | MODERN |
|------|-------------|--------|
| 1 | Paper | Clock |
| 2 | Cotton | China |
| 3 | Leather | Crystal, glass |
| 4 | Linen (silk) | Appliances |
| 5 | Wood | Silverware |
| 6 | Candy or iron | Wooden objects |
| 7 | Wool (copper) | Desk sets |
| 8 | Bronze | Linens, lace |
| 9 | Pottery (willow) | Leather goods |
| 10 | Tin, aluminum | Diamond |
| 11 | Steel | Fashion jewelry |
| 12 | Silk (linen) | Pearls, colored gems |
| 13 | Lace | Textiles, furs |
| 14 | Ivory | Gold jewelry |
| 15 | Crystal | Watches |
| 16 | Silver | Hollowware |
| 17 |  | Furniture |
| 18 |  | Porcelain |
| 19 |  | Bronze |
| 20 | China | Platinum |
| 21 |  | Brass, nickel |
| 22 |  | Copper |
| 23 |  | Silver plate |
| 24 |  | Musical instruments |
| 25 | Silver | Sterling silver |
| 26 |  | Original artwork |
| 27 |  | Sculpture |
| 28 |  | Orchids |
| 29 |  | New furniture |
| 30 | Pearl | Diamond |
| 31 |  | Timepieces |
| 32 |  | Conveyances/ automobiles |
| 33 |  | Amethyst |
| 34 |  | Opal |
| 35 | Coral (jade) | Jade |
| 40 | Ruby | Ruby |
| 45 | Sapphire | Sapphire |
| 50 | Gold | Gold |

## MAID OR MATRON OF HONOR, BRIDESMAIDS

*Dear _____,*

*I can't believe this moment has finally arrived. Do you remember looking up at the stars and thinking, "somewhere the man I will marry is looking at these stars, too, but where is he?!" In the blink of an eye, it seems, that moment arrived. We sure kissed a lot of frogs to find the real princes. I want to thank you for always being there for me every single time my heart broke or I cried with joy—you helped bring me to this moment. I treasure our friendship and thank you for standing beside me on my very special wedding day.*

*Love you,*

_____

### GRATEFUL SAGE TIP

Don't think that once you're married the romance
is over. It's up to you to keep it alive.

"*May you always walk in sunshine. May you never want for more. May Irish angels rest their wings beside your nursery door.*"

—IRISH BLESSING

# CHAPTER 9

## THANK YOU, BABY!

## BABY SHOWERS, CHRISTENINGS, AND FIRST BIRTHDAYS

There is no single moment in your life more exciting than finding out you are expecting a baby. In that split second, a tiny heartbeat will change your world forever, and nothing will ever be the same again. Whatever your beliefs are, know that life is a gift we are universally thankful for, and when the miracle of birth is given to you, never take for granted the blessings you have been given from above. How you announce your child to the world is significant, too, as that child's presence has an impact that reaches past your own life and touches the hearts of not only your family and friends, but the world.

### WE'RE HAVING A BABY— ANNOUNCEMENTS AND SOCIAL MEDIA

Congratulations! It's time to announce your good news. Thanks to the digital empire we now live in, there are dozens of wonderfully creative ways to let your loved ones know you have a pea in the pod. Here are some ideas and guidelines to help as you spread your joy:

* Even though you are bursting with the baby secret, remember that some parents wait about three months to announce a pregnancy before publicly sharing.

❋ Typically, birth announcements are personally shared, but today, there are some spectacular ways to reveal on social media that you have a bun in the oven. From posting a picture of your ultrasound, to sharing an image of you and your partner holding a chalkboard sign with the phrase "1 + 2 = 3," to countless other ideas, mommies have shared their heartfelt ideas online. Be inspired and create your own proclamation!

❋ Remember, you can use a stationery app to upload your picture and send your announcement via email, as a post on social media, or on a card through the mail with a stamp!

❋ Want to make it personal? Reach around the world and use a video chat app like Skype or FaceTime so you can be part of the life-changing moment with your loved ones.

❋ Really creative? Make a video and tell your story. That baby will cherish it for a lifetime.

## SOCIAL MEDIA DELIVERY ROOM NEWS— THE BROADCAST RULES

There is simply nothing more exciting than the birth of a sweet little baby and the thrill of sharing your good news. Before you head to the delivery room, define your social media rules with friends and family about how to help spread your joy to the world! Here are a few ideas:

❋ Please wait to share the love on social media sites about our sweet little baby until we are ready to announce her/his arrival and give you permission to do so.

❋ Please wait to post pictures of the baby until we are ready to show them.

❋ Please wait to share the baby's name and details.

❋ Please wait before "checking in" on social media with your GPS location at the hospital, so our privacy is protected.

Remember, if you want to keep as much of the details as private as possible, turn on your privacy settings.

## Do's and Don'ts for Expectant Moms

1. Do pick up or order your thank-you note stationery and postage stamps online before your baby shower. When in doubt, remember that Crane & Co. is always an elegant and stylish choice for stationery.

2. Do ask someone at your shower to make a list of every gift you receive and write down who gave it.

3. Do consider picking up a nice name and address book to pass around so your guests can write down their current contact information.

4. Don't forget to send a thank-you note to the person who hosted the shower for you.

5. Do handwrite your notes and keep them looking as elegant and gracious as possible. Remember, these heartfelt thank-yous for your baby become treasured keepsakes.

6. Do remember to refer to "Thank-You Notes 101" for your thank-you note guidelines.

7. Do start writing and sending out your notes as soon as possible.

8. Don't *ever* use email to send out your baby thank-you notes. If you want to go the electronic route and send a digital thank-you, check out a stationery app like www.RedStamp.com, which allows you to write your personal thank-you note and upload an image, which it then sends out for you.

## A MOTHER'S INTUITION:
## PAY ATTENTION TO THE RED FLAGS

We are born with many senses. One of the most powerful is our gift of intuition. It's that feeling, that sense of knowing when something just doesn't seem right, or that nagging sensation of dread when you know someone isn't telling you the truth. Chances are your feelings are correct. Pay attention to these "red flags," trust that tiny voice, and really listen when a thought crosses your mind. A mother's intuition can save a life.

**Ten Things Every Grateful New Mom Should Know**

1. If you're ordering birth announcements, do an Internet search for adorable ways to announce your sweet pea and browse the cute mommy-to-be ideas on Pinterest or Instagram. Make sure you purchase your thank-you notes at the same time as your birth announcements. It's one less thing you'll have to worry about later on.

2. Trying to cut costs but want to update your status? Remember, you can send paper birth announcements to close friends and family to have as treasured keepsakes and send the balance of your announcements digitally via email or a social media post.

3. Just about everything—from personalized thank-you notes, photo postage stamps, ink pens, and even what you'll need for the baby—can be ordered online.

4. It's a good rule to send out your thank-you notes within two weeks, but if you miss the time frame, add something like, "With the sleepless nights of our precious new baby, all the days have rolled into one . . ."

5. After the baby is born, it's likely more presents and flowers will arrive. Even though everyone understands that you just had a baby, they still expect a thank-you note.

6. If you receive a bouquet of flowers, it's always a good idea to call the person who sent them, so you match the same level of enthusiasm with which the flowers were sent. If you aren't up to it, then have your husband or a friend call on your behalf. If you get flowers in the hospital, make sure you bring the gift cards home with you so you won't forget to send a note later.

7. Remember to wait before removing the tags on baby clothes and keep gift receipts until after the baby is born in case you need to make exchanges. If you can't return or exchange the gifts, consider donating the items to a charity that can give them to people who really need them.

8. Keep the gift cards and note the item on the back of each. Mark it with a check or star when you've sent your thank-you note and put the gift cards in your baby box.

9. Make sure to thank all the people in your life who went through your pregnancy with you—and put up with you during your mood swings and midnight cravings, too. And if you're adopting, thank all the people who helped bring that little miracle into your arms.

10. Always remember the importance of your health and your baby's. Don't let your thank-you notes stress you out. If you are feeling overwhelmed, write one a day until they are finished. Keep in mind that having a baby isn't an everyday occurrence, so cherish this time—it passes far too quickly.

*May there be a generation of children*
*on the children of your children.*

—IRISH BLESSING

## MASTERING BABY THANK-YOUS!

When you're getting ready to welcome a new addition to the family, the demands of pregnancy and preparing for a baby can make it difficult just to keep up with your busy schedule. In addition, there are hundreds of thank-you notes to write before, during, and after the baby for months to come. Just when you think you've received your last gift and sent off your final thank-you note, you get another present! Still, it's important to let your friends and family know how much you appreciate their love, support, and generosity during this special time. So if you're expecting or adopting, here are some suggestions and sample thank-yous to help you express your gratitude and still keep your strength.

## BABY SHOWER THANK-YOUS—SAMPLE NOTES

BABY BOOK OR PHOTO ALBUM

*Dear _____,*

*Your presence at my shower was a gift in itself. Thank you for the gorgeous (baby book/photo album). I am really looking forward to filling the pages and capturing every single moment the baby does anything. Thank you again for all your love and support.*

*With my love,*

_____

## BABY/VIDEO MONITOR

Dear _____,

It was so thoughtful of you to send us a gift for (baby's name). I had no idea I would be so nervous each and every single time I stepped out of the baby's room for fear I wouldn't hear (him/her/them) crying. Having your gift of a baby monitor has given me the freedom to do normal daily things like take a shower! Now my mind is at ease, knowing I will be able to (listen /see) my little one(s) and be there when (he/she/they) need(s) me, no matter where I am in the house! Thank you!

Sincerely yours,

_____

## BLANKET

Dear _____,

I absolutely adore the beautiful (satin/cotton/muslin) receiving blanket and am looking forward to using it. I still can't believe that very soon I will have a cute little bundle of joy! Thank you so much for such a lovely and thoughtful gift to snuggle the baby in. I know the baby will love it as much as I do.

With love,

_____

## CAR SEAT

*Dear _____,*

*What a thoughtful gift you gave me. Just think, the very first thing the baby will be nestled in as (he/she/they) leave(s) the hospital for a safe journey home is your car seat. Thank you for the one thing I needed most! Even more important, thank you for being with me at my shower. Your presence made the day that much more special to me.*

*With affection,*

_____

## CLOTHING

*Dear _____,*

*I just want to thank you again for the beautiful things you gave us for (baby's name). They are all lovely and certainly arrived in the nick of time. She is already wearing the (name of item), dripping milk all over herself, and quite honestly being the most beautiful baby I could have ever wished for. Thank you so much for thinking of us; we really appreciate it. Please send our love to (name of spouse/partner/relative).*

*Love,*

_____

## FILL IN THE BLANKS

Dear _____,

What an incredible surprise it was to open the front door this afternoon and find a big box addressed to the baby. I love the (name of item)! That was definitely one thing I absolutely needed to have for our little one. Thank you for such a thoughtful gift for our sweet pea.

With love,

_____

## GRANDPARENTS

Dear Mom,

I just want to thank you for all the help and advice you have given me with the baby. Knowing you are there to lend a shoulder to cry on and answer my call for help in the middle of the night when the baby is crying . . . well, screaming, . . . has been a godsend for me. I only hope I am as wonderful a parent as you have been to me. I love you and thank you always.

Love,

_____

P.S. When can you babysit?

## MONEY, STOCK, SAVINGS BONDS

Dear _____,

Thank you so much for your generous check for the baby. We have decided to (put it in/open up) the baby's savings account. Please know it will be put to good use and help ensure (him/her) a good education. Thank you for your thoughtfulness and for giving our little one just what (he/she) needed.
With much love,

_____

## STROLLER

Dear _____,

Oh, you shouldn't have, but we are so thankful you did! We love the (brand name) stroller for the baby. It will take us from the baby stages all the way past those toddler years and then some! Now I will be able to stroll (down the avenue/through the mall) and shop while my little one relaxes in total luxury. Thank you so much! I love it!
With affection,

_____

## SHOWER HOSTESS—FROM THE MOMMY TO BE

Dear _____,

Words cannot express how much I appreciate your giving me a baby shower. It was truly the best party I have ever been to. From the tiny party favors to the delicious pink and blue cupcakes, everything was simply perfect. Thank you for making me feel so wonderful. I am blessed to have you in my life.
Love,

_____

Dear _____,

*I want to thank you for including me in your beautiful celebration for (name of mommy) and her forthcoming bundle of joy. I know I speak for everyone in saying that we all had a wonderful time and truly enjoyed spending time in your lovely home. You are truly a gracious hostess, and it was a pleasure to be part of the festivities. Thank you so very much.*

*Sincerely yours,*

_____

## CHRISTENING—SAMPLE NOTES

When you're celebrating baby's christening, here are some heavenly notes to help you show your appreciation for baby's blessings.

Dear _____,

*What an honor it was to have you celebrate (baby's name) christening with us. We were simply thrilled when we opened your gift. Please know the (name of gift) is something that we are certain the baby will cherish for a lifetime. Thank you for your kindness and blessings.*

*Love,*

_____

*Dear _____,*

*Thank you so very much for joining my family to celebrate my special christening day. I simply adore the (name of gift) you gave me and I will think of all of you every time I (see it/use it). More important, I so appreciate all of the love and support you have given to my family. From my little heart, I thank you. May God bless you and your family.*

*With love,*

_____

---

OFFICIATING PRIEST, REVEREND, OR FATHER

---

*Dear _____,*

*You are indeed a very special and holy man to us. We want you to know that you have affected not only our lives but also the lives of the families in our (church/parish) community. We are so grateful to you for the service you have given in God's name. We humbly thank you for initiating our child into God's divine grace through baptism and welcoming him into the church.*

*Yours faithfully,*

_____

## GRATEFUL SAGE TIP

Traditionally, when sending notes, letters, or general correspondence to a member of the clergy, you would use a closing such as "Respectfully yours" or "Faithfully yours."

## FIRST BIRTHDAYS—SAMPLE NOTES

Baby's first birthday is always an exciting event as we look back on the first year of this incredible little life and know we will cherish those moments forever. Here you'll find a few thank-you notes you can copy, modify, or use as your own to help you focus on the real blessings in your life—your baby!

### ARTS AND CRAFTS

*Dear _____,*

*It was so wonderful to see you at my birthday party. I really enjoyed opening your present and discovering the (arts and crafts item) you gave me! As a matter of fact, I am already making fabulous things, and my mother is delighted I am working on my creativity—as long as I'm outside. Thank you for such an imaginative gift!*

*With affection,*

*_____*

### FILL IN THE BLANKS

*Dear _____,*

*I just want to thank you for coming to my birthday party. It was so wonderful to have you there to celebrate with me. I love the (name of gift) you gave me. It is the perfect thing for me to play with!*

*Thank you for your thoughtfulness.*

*Sincerely,*

*_____*

*Dear _____,*

*Thank you for celebrating my first birthday with me. I really appreciate the (name of gift) you gave me, too. It was the one thing I wanted and I look forward to playing with it every day! I appreciate your generosity. Please let my mom know when we can set up a playdate!*

*Your friend,*

_____

*Dear _____,*

*You can't imagine my excitement when I opened your gift! I love the (name of gift) and am already enjoying playing with it. Thank you so much for your generosity and for thinking of me on my birthday.*

*Love,*

_____

## GIFT CARDS

*Dear _____,*

*What a pleasure it was to have you celebrate my birthday with me. I loved the gift cards you gave me, too! I look forward to going shopping and picking out all my favorite things. Thank you for a very special gift.*

*With affection,*

_____

## TEDDY BEAR

Dear _____,

*I could barely contain myself as I ripped the tissue off your present*
*to find out what was inside. I was so excited when I saw a little*
*(color of bear) ear sticking out . . . I just knew I had a new best friend!*
*I want you to know that "Teddy" and I are crazy about each other.*
*Oops, have to go . . . he's in the kitchen looking for the honey!*
*Thank you!*

_____

### GRATEFUL SAGE TIP

It's a good idea to pass along the gift of gratitude
to your children and teach them how to send their
own thank-you notes once they're able to write.

*Let gratitude be the pillow upon which*
*you kneel to say your nightly prayer.*

—MAYA ANGELOU, AMERICAN POET AND NOVELIST

"*To speak gratitude is courteous and pleasant, to enact gratitude is generous and noble, but to live gratitude is to touch Heaven.*"

—JOHANNES A. GAERTNER, GERMAN AUTHOR AND POET

# CHAPTER 10

## BELATED THANKS AND GESTURES OF APPRECIATION

## IT'S NEVER TOO LATE TO SAY THANK YOU

Even gracious guys and dolls get so wrapped up in the swirl of life that we put off sending thank-you notes. As the weeks rush by, we find ourselves worrying about our tardiness and wondering how we can ever say thank you now that so much time has passed. There are also those occasions when we realize how influential the kindness of a teacher really was or how essential the deep loyalty of a friend, and we wish we could turn back the clock so we could thank that person properly for making a difference in our lives. The good news is—it's never too late to say thank you.

### WRITING THE BELATED THANK-YOU NOTE

The format of your thank-you note should match the formality of the event or spirit in which the gift, favor, or kindness was given. Weddings typically require a formal note of thanks, as do social occasions. Just because your note is late is no reason to skip appropriate etiquette. Handwritten notes are always preferred, and if your thank-you is late to the point of embarrassment, avoid sending an email. If you were going to send an email thank-you note, you wouldn't have been so late in doing it! So take a minute, sit down, and write that thank-you!

## Ten Good Reasons Why It's Never Too Late to Say Thank You

1. Because it's never too late to thank someone for making a difference in your life.

2. Because it's the right thing to do!

3. Because everyone wants to feel appreciated.

4. Because even late thank-yous are powerful, especially when the gift giver thinks the gift or gesture is forgotten.

5. Because sometimes people have no idea how meaningful their life's contributions have been to you until you tell them.

6. Because the gift of gratitude has the ability to affect people's lives, no matter how late it is.

7. Because not saying thank you can damage your relationship and reputation.

8. Because the unthanked person may stop giving to you and others.

9. Because people will remember the kind of person you were long after you're gone.

10. Because a late thank-you is better than none at all.

## Six Do's and Don'ts for Tardy Thank-Yous

1. Do send your thank-you note as soon as you remember so you don't forget again.

2. Don't ever say you were too busy to thank someone for thinking of you.

3. Do try to capture the same excitement you felt when you received the gift or gesture.

4. Don't belabor the apologies for your tardiness in your note.

5. Do keep your note upbeat.

6. Do refer to "Thank-You Notes 101" while writing your thank-yous!

## QUIPS FROM GRATEFUL SAGES
## THROUGH THE AGES

*Just to be is a blessing. Just to live is holy.*
—RABBI ABRAHAM JOSHUA HESCHEL, JEWISH THEOLOGIAN

*In the end, we will remember not the words of our enemies, but the silence of our friends.*
—DR. MARTIN LUTHER KING JR.,
AMERICAN CIVIL RIGHTS LEADER

*At times our own light goes out and is rekindled by a spark from another person. Each of us has cause to think with deep gratitude of those who have lighted the flame within us.*
—ALBERT SCHWEITZER, NOBEL LAUREATE

*Silent gratitude isn't much use to anyone.*
—GLADYS BRONWYN STERN, ENGLISH NOVELIST

*O Lord that lends me life, lend me a heart replete with thankfulness!*
—WILLIAM SHAKESPEARE, ELIZABETHAN POET AND
PLAYWRIGHT, *KING HENRY VI*

### GRATEFUL SAGE TIP

"The Bag of a Million Thank-Yous." A wonderful way to acknowledge an important person or teacher in your life is to initiate a box, bag, or scrapbook filled with thank-you notes from friends, parents, students, and faculty. This kind of gift is a priceless keepsake.

## IT'S NEVER TOO LATE TO SAY THANK YOU—SAMPLE NOTES

We've heard our parents say a million times over, "Did you send a thank-you note?" That simple reminder conjures up panic and fear to the point that, for many of us, the grateful feeling for the gift is lost and the thank-you note forgotten. So for all you thank-you procrastinators, here are some belated thank-you notes that will help you recapture the moment and let the people in your past know you are grateful for their generosity.

THANK YOU FOR BEING MY MENTOR

*Dear* _____,

*There are no words to express how grateful I am to you for being my mentor. Thank you for sharing with me your life and your hard-earned wisdom. I am so tremendously appreciative. I only hope that one day I can repay the honor.*

*Sincerely,*

_____

*Dear* _____,

*For years, I have admired your work not only as a talented business (man/woman) but also as a gracious philanthropist in our community. Through your tireless dedication, you have shown me how essential it is in life to love what you do and never, ever settle for less than what you deserve. Thank you for lighting my way.*

*Gratefully yours,*

_____

## THANK YOU, OLD FRIEND

*Dear _____,*

*So many times I think of you and the time we spent together. I wish we could walk back in time, even if only for a moment, and be (age) again. Thank you for being my friend during the good, bad, and in-between. Please know that no matter where life takes us, I will never forget how wonderful you were to me. I wish you love and happiness.*

*Gratefully yours,*

_____

## THANK YOU, TEACHER OR ROOM PARENT

*Dear _____,*

*What a wonderful year we have had together! I wanted to take a moment to thank you for your dedication throughout the year. I know firsthand how hard you worked to finish each special project for the children, and their eyes glowed with such excitement every time you created something wonderful for them. Please know you have left an indelible mark on their memories that they will treasure for a lifetime. Thank you a million times!*

*With sincere appreciation,*

_____

## THANK YOU, TEACHER

*Dear Ms. _____,*

*This "Bag of a Million Thank-Yous" is filled with thank-you notes from the faculty, children, and their parents, all of whom were quite taken with the love, creativity, and tireless dedication you gave to your class and our school. Thank you for giving our precious children memories that will last a lifetime. We salute and applaud your tireless efforts.*

*Sincerely yours,*

_____


## THANK YOU FOR THE GIFT

*Dear _____,*

*Although I thanked you in person for the (name of gift) you gave me, I want you to know how sincerely grateful I am to you for your thoughtfulness. In fact, every time I see it I think of you and how blessed I am to have you in my life. Thank you for thinking of me.*

*Sincerely yours,*

_____

*Dear _____,*

*I have no excuse! Regardless of my tardiness, I absolutely loved the*
*(name of gift) you sent me. Now that I have it, I don't know how I*
*ever survived without it. Thank you so very much for taking the time*
*to find me the perfect gift.*
*With my appreciation,*

_____

## THANK YOU FOR MAKING A DIFFERENCE IN MY LIFE

*Dear _____,*

*There are times in our lives when we are utterly unaware of the effect we*
*have on someone else. I don't know what I would have done without you.*
*There are simply no words to express how grateful I am to you for your*
*kindness, loyalty, love, and selflessness. You have a lifelong friend in me.*
*With my sincere thanks,*

_____

*Dear Mr. _____,*

*There is no way I could go back in time and thank you for everything. But*
*I have this moment. I humbly thank you, from the bottom of my heart to*
*the heavens above, for making a difference in my life. I am forever grateful.*
*Yours truly,*

_____

## THANK YOU, DAD

*Dear Dad,*

*You are the kind of father every girl dreams of having. Beyond compare, you are the kind of man by which others are measured. You are intelligent, accomplished, creative, and handsome—I am so blessed to call you my father. Thank you for always being there and loving me. I adore you.*

*Love,*

---

### GRATEFUL SAGE TIP

Did you know that Crane & Co. has been around since 1776, when Stephen Crane's mill sold Paul Revere the paper to issue the first Colonial banknotes? To this day, Crane & Co. manufactures the paper for much of our worldwide currency. www.Crane.com.

## THANK YOU, MOM

*Dear Mom,*

*Thank you for making me do the things I didn't want to do, because they were good for me. Thank you for having the wisdom and patience to let me make mistakes I could learn from. Thank you for encouraging me to finish school when I wanted to see the world. Thank you for holding me through every broken heart. Thank you for making me the woman I am today. Thank you for being my mother. I love you so much.*

*Love,*

———————

*Feeling gratitude and not expressing it*
*is like wrapping a present and not giving it.*

—WILLIAM ARTHUR WARD, AMERICAN WRITER AND POET

*I know in my heart that man is good. That what is right will always eventually triumph. And there is a purpose and worth to each and every life.*

—RONALD REAGAN,
FORTIETH UNITED STATES PRESIDENT AND PEACEMAKER

# CHAPTER 11

## FAREWELL, MY FRIEND

## FOR YOUR KINDNESS AND SYMPATHY—THANK YOU FROM THE HEART

There comes a time in all our lives when we must say good-bye to a loved one or dear friend. Whether the departure is anticipated or unexpected, it is one of the most heart-wrenching moments we may ever have to endure. It is the support, love, and sympathy we receive from our friends and family that help us make it through the day when we feel as if we can't go on. With the help of friends and loved ones, we eventually heal, and over time we are able to laugh again without bursting into tears. Remember, life is a journey, and the people we meet along the way may be there for only a moment, but they linger in our hearts forever, never to be forgotten. It is important that we show appreciation to the people who are so meaningful in our lives while we have the chance to do so. Then, when the time does come to say farewell, we feel satisfied in knowing that the person we loved so dearly knew it and was recognized.

### WRITING THE SYMPATHY THANK-YOU NOTE

The moment will come when you are ready to write your thank-you notes for the support you received following the passing of a loved one. All of the basic rules of writing thank-you notes apply; however, there are no restrictions on sending them by a certain time.

It's best to keep formality and elegance in your notes as you honor the departed. Remember, too, that many of the people you are writing your thank-you notes to are also grieving. Thank-yous should be sent to everyone who helped you get through this period of time, including clergy and anyone who sent a gift or condolence card, served as a pallbearer, provided assistance, sent flowers, or made a financial contribution or donation to charity in your loved one's memory.

## Ten Sympathetic Sage Tips

1. Do have someone help you if you are unable to write the thank-you notes yourself.

2. Do include the deceased's memorial card in your thank-you note. It is a special keepsake for the people who couldn't attend the memorial or funeral. These can be easily ordered through the funeral home.

3. Do send a personal, handwritten thank-you for flowers, charity donations, financial contributions, meals, or just shoulders you cried on.

4. Do check into the preprinted and personalized sympathy thank-you cards that are available in stationery stores or online.

5. Do write a few words of personal thanks in preprinted sympathy thank-you cards.

6. Don't send emailed sympathy thank-you notes if you can avoid it, as they aren't as personal as handwritten notes.

7. Do consider sending sympathy acknowledgment cards if the loved one who passed away was a prominent person.

8. Do consider a publishing tribute to the deceased in your local newspaper when a public acknowledgment is necessary.

9. Don't hesitate to send a condolence note to a friend who's suffered the loss of a friend or family member. Expressions of sympathy are always appropriate.

10. Do make a post on social media to thank everyone who sent you their love and prayers electronically.

## ONLINE CONDOLENCES: USING SOCIAL MEDIA

The Internet has become the digital language in which we instantaneously and simultaneously communicate to maintain our human relationships. Holding up an electronic candle to the world, we stand united in a global cause or in the passing of a loved one or legend who affected us all. Social media sites give us a voice to share, grieve, and record memories that connect our hearts. To post or not to post, that is indeed the question when announcing to friends and family that your loved one's soul has passed on to spirit. Here are some tips to help you honor the dearly departed.

* Use social media to ask for positive thoughts, energy, and prayers to be sent to your loved one and family to help them through this difficult time.

* Remember, social media is a public bulletin board. Before you post a funeral notice on these sites, do make sure to notify by phone the people in that person's inner circle who are the most affected by the passing and to get their approval.

* If you post a celebration of life announcement, be sure to include the date, time, location of service, and reception links, and also let everyone know if the family is requesting a charity donation in lieu of flowers.

* Remember, while email is more personal than social media, a phone call is still the preferred method to express your condolences.

* Many funeral homes have an "online condolence" website set up, a central place to collect well wishes and share memories of your loved one. The entries people write and share can then be sent to you by email or assembled into a keepsake book.

* Make a post on social media or by email to create a "meal train" to help organize donations of food and desserts. Then everyone can feel they are helping the bereaved in some small way.

## PAY IT FORWARD WITH LOVE AND HONOR

### GRATITUDE IN ACTION

The next time you say farewell to someone you love, start a new tradition. Ask your friends and loved ones to write a note or letter about what that person meant to them. It could be a few words or even a story. Keep the notes together or make a treasured memorial book. Long after the flowers have faded and people have returned to their lives, you will cherish these memories for a lifetime.

## SPIRIT ANIMALS—
## AMBASSADORS OF GOODWILL

Our animals are ambassadors of goodwill that enrich our lives, listen to our stories, and witness our triumphs and failures with unconditional love. Like little beacons of light, our silky felines, gracious canines, and noble steeds are loyal companions that look into our eyes and make us feel loved. When we must bid them adieu, it is just as difficult as saying good-bye to a family member, because they are. If you have been touched by a spirit animal that has filled your heart and touched your soul, remember the animal by making a donation in its memory to help save another animal, contacting your local pet rescue group and adopting, or simply sending love to other animals with a kind word, thought, or pat on the head as you pass by. Extending your condolences to a friend who has lost their very best friend will be so appreciated. Know that your kindness will be rewarded.

*If all the beasts were gone, men would die from a great loneliness of spirit, for whatever happens to the beasts also happens to the man. All things are connected. Whatever befalls the Earth befalls the sons of the Earth.*

—CHIEF SEATTLE OF THE SUQUAMISH TRIBE,
LETTER TO PRESIDENT FRANKLIN PIERCE

## QUIPS FROM SYMPATHETIC SAGES THROUGH THE AGES

*May the road rise to meet you.*
*May the wind be always at your back.*
*May the sun shine warm upon your face*
*And rains fall soft upon your fields.*
*And until we meet again,*
*May God hold you in the hollow of His hand.*

—IRISH BLESSING

*Our life is made by the death of others.*

—LEONARDO DA VINCI, ITALIAN RENAISSANCE MAN

*It is worth dying to find out what life is.*

—T. S. ELIOT, ENGLISH POET AND NOBEL LAUREATE

*The boundaries between life and death are at best shadowy and*
*vague. Who shall say where one ends and where the other begins?*

—EDGAR ALLAN POE, AMERICAN WRITER AND POET

*Don't cry because it's over. Smile because it happened.*

—DR. SEUSS, AMERICAN WRITER AND CARTOONIST

## INTERNATIONAL CUSTOMS FOR HONORING THE DEARLY DEPARTED

Not all cultures regard death as a sad occasion. Some celebrate it as an exciting event that is part of the circle of life.

* ✻ Ancient Egyptians revered death because it began the journey to the afterlife. Considerable time and effort were spent in the preparation of funeral chambers to house the deceased's mummified body, supplies, food, weapons, jewels, sacred pets, and furniture so the soul would be prepared for its next life.

* ✻ Irish culture—steeped in myth and lore—celebrates the departed one's life with a "wake" prior to burial. With plenty of dancing and merrymaking, those at the wake make a last-ditch effort to wake up the deceased and confuse evil spirits that might be lurking nearby.

* ✻ Jewish law is legendary for celebrating life and for communally embracing the bereaved by surrounding them for seven days—the weeklong period when the mourners are "sitting shiva"—with food and comfort. During this important time of grieving, laughter, and reminiscing, mourners are reminded that life is for the living.

* ✻ In Mexico and other Central and South American countries, the living celebrate their deceased relatives on *"El Dia de los Muertos,"* or the *"Day of the Dead."* This pre-Columbian custom celebrates death as the passage to a new life.

## THANK-YOU ACKNOWLEDGMENTS

If you are interested in printing your own acknowledgment cards, here are some examples of what the phrasing should look like. Center the words on the card. Remember to include a handwritten personal note of thanks, too.

*The family of*
*(name of deceased)*
*acknowledges with deep appreciation your*
*kind expression of sympathy.*

---

*We will forever cherish the life of*
*(name of deceased)*
*and eternally wave to the heavens as (he/she)*
*begins (his/her) journey among the stars.*

---

*Our family sincerely thanks you for your*
*sympathy and thoughtfulness.*
*(name of widow/widower/family name)*
*gratefully acknowledges your loving expression*
*of sympathy during this sorrowful time of mourning.*

### GRATEFUL SAGE TIP
Crane & Co. makes it easy to purchase personalized and generic sympathy acknowledgment cards, memorial cards, and stationery online at www.Crane.com.

## FOR YOUR KINDNESS AND SYMPATHY— THANK YOU FROM THE HEART— SAMPLE NOTES

Here are a few notes to help you show your friends and family how much you appreciate their sympathy.

THANK YOU ON BEHALF OF THE FAMILY

*Dear _____,*

*On behalf of my (mother, father, grandparent, family), please accept (her/his/their) sincere thanks for the (card, letter, flowers, food, financial contribution, or other gift) you sent in memory of (name of deceased). It is only the generosity of good friends like you that has gotten us through this very difficult time. Thank you.*

*Respectfully yours,*

_____

THANK YOU FOR YOUR CHARITABLE DONATION

*Dear _____,*

*I know how much (name of deceased) treasured your friendship. If there was anyone in this world (he/she) loved and respected, it was you. Thank you for honoring (him/her) with your generous charitable donation to (name of charity). I am certain (he/she) would be so proud.*

*With my sincere appreciation,*

_____

## THANK YOU, CLERGY

*Dear _____,*

*This is definitely a moment in my life when I feel I am being tested by God. It seems so unfair for our loved ones to pass. While I am certain that (name of deceased) is in a better place, it has been so painful to say good-bye with grace and dignity. Thank you for helping me grieve, laugh, and cry. Thank you for showing me how to heal. God bless you.*

*Faithfully yours,*

_____

## THANKS FOR YOUR EXPRESSION OF SYMPATHY

*Dear _____,*

*There are simply no words to thank you for the loving expression of sympathy you have given us during the passing of (name of deceased). We are deeply grateful.*

*With our love,*

_____

## THANK YOU FOR THE FLOWERS OR FUNERAL WREATH

*Dear _____,*

*Your love and support during this tremendously difficult time are so greatly appreciated. The gorgeous white flowers you sent were spectacular, and I know that (name of deceased) would have loved them. On behalf of my family, I thank you.*

*Gratefully yours,*

_____

## THANK YOU FOR THE FOOD

Dear _____,

I understand you are grieving just as deeply as we are. Please know how much we appreciated the (food item) you brought us. It was absolutely delicious and we know it was made with all of your love. Thank you for taking the time to comfort us.

Sincerely yours,

_____

## THANK YOU FOR THE LOVING TRIBUTE

Dear _____,

My (mother/father/other family member/name of deceased) was the light of our life. Thank you for honoring (him/her) with your loving tribute. We are forever grateful for the heartwarming memories you have shared with us, and we will treasure them for a lifetime.

Love,

_____

*May the Force be with you . . .*

—GEORGE LUCAS, SCREENWRITER, *STAR WARS*

# INDEX